Deconstructing Purity Culture to Embrace Sexual Pleasure

Deconstructing Purity Culture to Embrace Sexual Pleasure

Andreya Jones

ROWMAN & LITTLEFIELD
Lanham • Boulder • New York • London

Published by Rowman & Littlefield
An imprint of The Rowman & Littlefield Publishing Group, Inc.
4501 Forbes Boulevard, Suite 200, Lanham, Maryland 20706
www.rowman.com

86-90 Paul Street, London EC2A 4NE

British Library Cataloguing in Publication Information available

Library of Congress Cataloging-in-Publication Data available

ISBN 9798881800284 (cloth)
ISBN 9798881800291 (paperback)
ISBN 9798881800307 (ebook)

♾™ The paper used in this publication meets the minimum requirements of American National Standard for Information Sciences—Permanence of Paper for Printed Library Materials, ANSI/NISO Z39.48-1992.

To my children, Cassel and Briley, may you learn to embrace your bodies, your pleasure, and your sexuality without shame. I have worked and will continue to work diligently to break the toxic cycles in our culture so that you may grow up in a world where you have the freedom to be your authentic selves and love whomever you desire. Loving you is my greatest joy.

Contents

Introduction   ix

Part I   **1**

1   My Story   3

2   Who Is This For?   19

3   History of Evangelicalism and Purity Culture   29

4   Women in Purity Culture   35

5   Shame   39

6   Sexual Dysfunction   43

7   LGBTQIA+ and Purity Culture   57

Part II: Moving Into the Curriculum   **61**

8   Class 1: Origins of Purity Culture   63

9   Class 2: Shame and Guilt   77

10   Class 3: Religious Shame Around Sexuality   83

11   Class 4: Sexual Ethics   89

12   Class 5: Desire and Pleasure   99

13   Class 6: Masturbation and Self-Exploration   109

14   Class 7: Conclusion   123

15   Epilogue   129

Appendix: Informed Consent Form   131

References   137

Index   145

About the Author   153

Introduction

If you picked up this book, you may be someone who has lived through evangelical Christian purity culture, are curious about purity culture, or are working with or know someone from this population. The culture and messages of purity culture intersect and overlap between many religions and belief systems around the world. These religion-based movements prioritize abstinence outside of heterosexual marriage, virginity, and sexual purity. Members of these communities are taught that they will experience significant consequences and/or punishment if they do not abide by these rules and values, which often creates a sense of fear. Core beliefs around gender roles, purity of mind and body, virginity, power dynamics between men and women, and what is right or wrong in sexual behavior are a few of the topics that purity culture has strict rules about and beliefs around. The evangelical Christian church realized that controlling someone's sexuality gave them power and allowed them to better influence and control their members. Under the umbrella concept of purity culture, there are many different sects based on culture, gender, geographic location, and race. This book and curriculum can in no way address every single sect of purity culture. My focus is on the teachings and beliefs that came out of the white evangelical Christian church. I am aware that the teachings and beliefs of purity culture in Europe vary from those in Africa, which differ from those in the Middle East, and even those in the Black community in America. I also want to acknowledge that there are individuals who grew up in evangelical Christian purity culture who had a positive experience and do not struggle with their sexuality at all. It is my hope that no matter what sect of purity culture you come from or encounter, you will be able to find something of value in this book. I hope that you will discover some nugget of information that you can use to help bring healing to yourself or to others.

Part I

1

✝

My Story

I want to start off by saying that I acknowledge that I come from a place of privilege that impacts my views and how I move through the world. I am a white, cisgender, pansexual woman who has lived all over the world, speaks three languages, and had access to a higher level of education. I run a private relationship and sex therapy practice that allows me to live a comfortable life where I can provide for my children and my core needs are met. I know that my privilege affects the way I am viewed by others, the way that I show up in the world, and the lens through which I view life. I can only speak from my personal life experience, which I acknowledge is different from that of other people. For the individuals who flourished in the teachings of purity culture, I celebrate with you. I fully accept and understand that my experience is exactly that—my experience. I do not speak for everyone in this specific population. As a therapist, I focus on holding space for and validating the experiences and stories of every person who walks through my door. I work diligently to guide my clients on their path and never tell them what to think or do, or how to live. My privilege has given me access to many experiences and resources that others do not have access to.

I am extremely passionate about the topic of purity culture. While I have been on a journey of self-discovery and healing since 2003, it was not until 2019 that I really immersed myself into healing the pain and trauma that I experienced and have carried in my body for as long as I can remember. When I first began this journey of healing, I thought that I would reach a state of complete healing. Instead, what I have learned along the way is that healing is an ongoing process that is never truly complete.

Healing is not linear and there is no ultimate destination to be reached. The process of healing is like peeling an onion. I peel off one small layer only to find another layer underneath. Each layer is unique, varying in size, thickness, and potency. Each one of these layers helped form me into the woman I am today. It is unbelievably beautiful to wake up each day knowing that there is more to learn about myself and my story. I have the capacity to grow and change whenever and however I choose.

This journey of becoming is one that takes a lifetime. Embracing this reality has given me a sense of freedom. The pressure to be healed or "all better" is no longer something I wake up panicking about in the middle of the night. Instead, I have given myself permission to go at my own pace and process in whatever way feels best to me, knowing that as long as I keep showing up and sitting with the hard feelings, I am succeeding. The fear of failure is something that was ingrained in me from a very young age, having grown up in the conservative evangelical Christian community that I did. The focus on good and bad—right and wrong—failure and success are ones that I know all too well. When I find myself falling back into these old ways of thinking, I remind myself that the definition of failure I choose to embrace is that of not trying. As long as I show up, ask the hard questions, and make an effort, then I am succeeding on this journey.

I was born into and grew up in a conservative evangelical Christian community on the island of Papua New Guinea. I am the firstborn in a family of five that consists of my mom, dad, and two younger brothers. My parents met while they were overseas and found a deep connection with one another based on their desire to be missionaries. After getting married they moved to Papua New Guinea, where we lived on a fenced-in compound that was home to approximately 1,000 people. The primary focus of the organization that my parents worked for was to help translate the Bible into the traditional languages of the Papua New Guinean people. The mission of the organization that my parents worked for was to translate the Bible into as many languages as they could, to convert people into Christianity. With over 860 languages in the country of Papua New Guinea, this was quite a feat. To keep people focused on the mission, the organization implemented strict rules that if not followed could result in termination from the organization. By instilling fear in the community members, particularly the women and children, the organization was able to obtain compliance and order. While I know that the organization did not intentionally plan to harm its members, I do not believe that freedom of beliefs, values, or ideas was something they wanted to encourage or embrace. To join this organization, members had to go through an extensive interview process and had to sign an agreement that they would uphold and follow the rules and beliefs of the organization. In the case that the agreement was broken or not upheld, the organization had the right to discipline or remove the member(s) from the organization and from the life that they had built.

I was raised to believe that there was only one God and that the greatest gift we could give to God was to go minister to people about his word, his love, and his teachings. As a child I did not know any other way of life. I was raised to believe that we were all born sinful, the Bible was the ultimate truth, and that the only path to heaven was to give your life and heart to Jesus Christ. People who did not give their hearts and lives to Christ would be separated from God and ultimately go to hell. Our mission was to go to other countries and teach people about Jesus so we could save them from eternal damnation. Essentially our religion was the one and only true religion. It was us versus them. The fear of sinning and going to hell was one that I distinctly remember keeping me up at night as a child. I developed anxiety at a very young age because I was afraid to make a mistake or do something wrong that could possibly make God not love me. My entire world revolved around right and wrong—black and white. I now know that this is the way that the community guaranteed compliance, but it has made it very difficult for me to live in the real world now that I no longer live in that highly controlled religious community. There are a lot of grays in the world and that is a concept that I continue to struggle with even to this day. Through the help of therapy, I have learned to find more safety in flexibility and going with the flow. Giving myself permission to ask questions and determine what I believe or think without the influence of religion or fear is something I continue to focus on each day.

The topic of sexuality was rarely discussed in my community, which sent the message that there was something inherently wrong or sinful about sexuality. When a topic is avoided or not talked about by adults in a community, it leaves the children of the community to create narratives and beliefs about that topic. Often, these narratives are saturated in fear, confusion, and shame. This in turn leaves the children of the community in a place of vulnerability. A place where they can be taken advantage of, abused, manipulated, and traumatized. All of which happened to me.

My first memory of being sexually abused was when I was five years old. At the time I did not know that this was abuse because it was not discussed. My body knew that something was not right, and I was filled with fear that someone would find out what had happened. I assumed that I would be the one to be punished if my secret was uncovered, so I kept quiet. Growing up in Papua New Guinea and Senegal, West Africa, I was often surrounded by people who had never seen a white person before, let alone a little girl with blonde hair and blue eyes. Whenever we would go visit local towns or villages, the people would often touch my body and particularly my hair. It was normal for me to walk down the street or through the market while being touched by complete strangers the entire time. I grew up without bodily autonomy. I believed that other people had every right to touch me in whatever ways they wished. I did not understand the concept of consent because it was not something I was taught about and was not valued in my community. I had multiple experiences of sexual abuse throughout my childhood at the hands of community members who were part of the organization my parents worked for. There were multiple experiences with other children, as well as babysitters and adults in my community. I have no recollection of conversations about body safety, consent, or sexual abuse. I do, however, remember the messages about modesty, purity, and waiting to have sex until marriage. Many of the kids that I grew up with were not taught about their sexual anatomy, sex, or pleasure. I remember my mother reading me a book about sex when I was eight. The book stated that sex was a way for married people to express love and have babies. I remember that the picture in the book was of a man and a woman lying next to each other in bed covered by a blanket. I was fascinated by that picture. What were they doing under that blanket? So many questions were left unanswered, and I had no idea who I could go to for answers. I am grateful that my mother took the time to talk to me about sex in the way that she knew how. While it left me confused and curious, I had more knowledge than many of my friends.

In the community I grew up in, I was taught that any sexual expression outside of heterosexual marriage was a sin. The adults in my community were either single and celibate or married to someone of the opposite sex. No one in my community got divorced because divorce was also viewed as a sin, unless you were being physically abused. Being part of the LGBTQIA+ community was also sinful unless you chose not to act on your desires and remained celibate. I cannot remember anyone in my community identifying as part of the LGBTQIA+ community, let alone discussing any sort of same-sex attraction. As I look back now, I am sure that there were closeted individuals, but they knew that they would not be welcome in the community if they came out. My community believed that members from the LGBTQIA+ community chose that "lifestyle." Being same-sex attracted was a choice and was not in alignment with God's plan for relationships or marriage. God intended for men and women to be partnered for life and anything outside of that was against God's will. One of the first people to sexually abuse me was an older girl in my community. I carried a lot of confusion and shame about these incidents because we were both girls, which I believed was a sin. I was scared that God would not love me because of this awful sin I had been a part of. I was not able to see at the time that the abuse happened to me and was not my fault. I now look back with extreme empathy for that little girl. I wish

I could have protected her, and I wish she had been told that she didn't do anything wrong and that what people did to her was not acceptable. It was not her fault. I began exploring my body at a very young age due to the abuse that I had experienced. While it is developmentally typical for young children to explore their bodies, this was never discussed in my family. I felt that I had to hide it from my parents out of the fear that I would be punished. I now know that I was using pleasurable touch to soothe my fear and anxiety due to the abuse and lack of safety in my life.

During puberty, the focus was on modesty and dressing in a way that would not tempt the men or boys in the community. There was an underlying message given to us that men were visual creatures who couldn't help themselves when it came to desire and arousal. As women we needed to prioritize the sexual safety of these men by dressing and speaking in nonsexual and modest ways. We lived in a country where women were not supposed to show their thighs, legs, or buttocks. I was required to wear long skirts and dresses to hide my body and protect myself from the desires and wandering eyes of men. The sexual safety of myself and others was solely my responsibility.

Rape was a common part of the Papua New Guinean culture. There were quite a few women and girls who were raped from my community during the time that I lived in Papua New Guinea. These incidents were not discussed or explained to us, which created even more confusion and fear. As women, we were encouraged to not go outside alone after dark and to always have a man walk with us at night to be safe. As a child I would lie in bed at night creating escape plans in my mind in case someone broke into our home or tried to hurt me. There was a built-in cabinet above my bed that I practiced climbing into so that I could hide there if anyone broke into our home. I was certain no one would ever find me there. My body would shake while I laid in the bed at night listening to the sounds of the night outside of my window. There were many times when I was so scared that it felt difficult to breathe. We had guards who walked around the community with dogs and walkie-talkies each night. There were many times that I woke up to the sound of talking on walkie-talkies right outside my bedroom window. While the guards were supposed to help me feel safe, they were a constant reminder that my world was unsafe and that I needed to be protected. I did not feel safe at night and even as an adult I still struggle to be in the dark alone.

One time my friend and I went to a local town where they had some stores and a market. While we walked around shopping, we noticed two men who began to follow us. My friend and I were hyperaware of these two men and began to walk faster so we could get away. The faster we walked, the more intensely the men followed us until they caught up to us and grabbed my friend's arm. We broke free and ran as fast as we could back to the hotel that we had been staying at with our families. Two white girls running through a crowd of people being chased by two Papua New Guinean men. No one seemed to notice or care. I remember the panic I felt in my chest—was this the time I was going to get hurt? Why had I believed I could go out shopping in the middle of the day without a man present? If something happened to us, it would be our faults. I still struggle with social anxiety in crowds. I'm hyperaware of my surroundings and what people are doing. When men approach me in a crowd, I get very anxious and often have to quickly move away.

Time and time again I got the message that I needed men to protect me from the terrors of the world. Men were the head of the households, the protectors, and the spiritual leaders. If a boy wanted to date me, he had to meet with my father and discuss his intentions prior to receiving my father's blessing to date me. I was taught that my father was my protector until I got married, at which time this responsibility would be passed to my husband. While this concept was presented as something I should feel grateful for, it made me feel that safety came from men instead of from within myself. I believed that I needed a man to be whole.

Any form of erotic or sexual touch between boys and girls was unacceptable outside of marriage. Dancing (other than swing dancing in a group setting) was discouraged. Kissing or any form of sexual play was strictly off-limits. If you wanted to be alone with your significant other, you had to find hiding places, which reinforced the belief that whatever you were doing was wrong or sinful even though it was developmentally exactly what you were supposed to be doing or experiencing. When I was 17, someone from the community saw my boyfriend lean down and kiss me goodnight at the end of our date. This community member went straight to my mother to inform her of what I had done. My mother approached me after school the following day and proceeded to question me about my behavior. She informed me that my behavior was a direct representation of our family and my relationship with God. She began to cry as she questioned whether I was sexually active. I knew I wasn't having sex, but I did have a physical relationship with my boyfriend at the time. He was older than I was and had a lot more experience than I did. I was hurt and angry that someone had told my mother that we had kissed. My mother reminded me that my behavior had put our family at risk of being asked to leave our community. This would be devastating for my family. It was my responsibility to change my behavior and make better choices so that my family would not have to leave our home, our life, and our community. This reality created a sense of tremendous shame and guilt that I carried in my spirit and my body for years afterward. These completely normal and healthy parts of relational and sexual development that children and young adults are meant to experience were shamed and not accepted. There were adults in my community who refused to let me participate in school activities or extracurricular activities because I was known as someone who was not modest and immoral because I dated someone they did not approve of. I remember having to fight my way into being a part of the youth band with the youth pastor because he didn't believe I was a Christian because of the person I had dated the year prior. While I was eventually allowed to be a part of the band, I realized that who I was had been defined by the behaviors and choices of someone I had dated and not on my behavior or choices. While my boyfriend had made a lot of poor decisions and had not followed the strict rules of our community, I struggled to understand how his decisions were now my responsibility. Was I supposed to control what he did? I did not condone many of the choices he made, but I could see that we were two separate people. I was not a reflection of him, I was just his girlfriend. I often felt that there was something wrong with me. Why did I have the feelings, desires, and thoughts that I did? Why was it OK for other people to touch me and hurt me? Why were adults allowed to make decisions for my life based on assumptions that were not based in truth?

We had two days of sexual education in middle school. The focus was on general sexual anatomy, pregnancy, and menstruation. Our teacher told us that sex would most likely be painful and that it was only for people who were married. Waiting to have sex until marriage was one of the greatest gifts we could give our future husband and a way to respect ourselves and set us apart from the rest of the world. We briefly discussed the major sexually transmitted infections. We learned about a few forms of birth control, but were not told how to access birth control since we were not married and therefore not supposed to be sexually active. Birth control was only accessible for married individuals in our community since they were the only people who were supposed to be having sex. My classmates who were having sex in secret had to drive to a town located about 40 minutes away where they could purchase condoms. The topics of pleasure, same-sex attraction, and consent were not discussed in those two days of sexual education.

In middle school, a group of young adults came to Papua New Guinea for a week to talk about and promote abstinence before marriage. I believe this group was associated with the True Love Waits organization. Organizations and people from the outside rarely came to the community where I lived, so whenever they did there was always a lot of excitement. Everyone wanted to know what they were coming to talk about and wanted to get involved. Most of us only visited our home countries every four years, so we were always interested in learning about what was new and popular from people who came to visit. The members of the group were young, attractive Americans, who came to share their passion about purity and Jesus. Their main message was that remaining abstinent until marriage was cool—it was sexy. Abstinence was a choice that we could all make to show our love and commitment to our faith and to our future spouses. Their presentations consisted of Christian rock music, funny skits, and testimonials, all wrapped up with an altar call where individuals could commit their lives and/or purity to Jesus. I remember looking around the church as my peers and the members from my community sang at the top of their lungs, praising God with their hands in the air and their eyes closed. I found myself wondering why I didn't feel what they felt, why I didn't have that kind of passion or love for Jesus. I so desperately wanted to feel what everyone else was feeling. I wanted to fit in. The group from America brought True Love Waits rings with them that many of us purchased at the end of their visit. For me, it was about peer pressure. If my friends were going to wear these rings and if not having sex before marriage was the right thing to do, then I didn't want to stand out or be different. When the purity pledge cards were passed around to everyone in the crowd I watched as my peers eagerly signed their names, with tears in their eyes and joy on their faces. The adults in the community beamed with pride as they watched the next generation commit themselves to abstinence. When I received my pledge card, I pretended to fill it out, but never actually wrote anything on it. There was no way I was going to make a promise to God or myself that I knew I had no intention of keeping. I knew that I wanted to experience sex outside of marriage because I wanted to make sure that whoever I married was sexually compatible with me. While I knew that sex outside of marriage was not part of the fairy tale I had been taught, there was part of me that doubted the truth of that fairy tale. I knew that my peers would not understand or be receptive to these thoughts or ideas, so like so many other things in my life, I kept quiet and hid my true self away. I wore my True Love Waits ring until I graduated from high school and moved to America. In my late twenties I found that ring in a box that had been in storage. I tried it on, and it still fit. I thought back to that teenager who had worn it to fit in. If only she had believed that her voice mattered. How I wished that she could've been free to ask questions and embrace her truth. I took off the ring and proudly threw it away. I made a commitment to myself that I would never again follow the crowd to fit in. Instead, I would ask the hard questions and be myself, even if that meant I would not be accepted by the people I loved.

In high school I found myself attracted to a few of my female friends, which was something I never told anyone out of fear that I would be judged and punished for having sinful desires or thoughts. I told myself that I just loved these girls as friends and that God had a husband for me who would come into my life in God's perfect timing. Getting married and having children was highly valued by people in my community. I remember dreaming about marriage and becoming a mom. At one point I wanted to have six children I could homeschool. I fantasized about the perfect husband and about how he would treat me and love me. I believed that if I followed God's word and the rules of my community, I would be rewarded with a man of God. A man who would treat me like a princess and would be my protector. I took all my same-sex attraction and put it in a box and hid it far away in the back of my mind. I chose to focus on finding the husband I was told God had in store for me so that I could lead a fulfilling life.

When I graduated from high school, I left the conservative community where I had been sheltered from divorce, the LGBTQIA+ community, and sexual expression. I flew the 36 hours back to America, where I started my freshman year at a small Christian college outside of Philadelphia, with peers who had grown up in a completely different world. I often felt lost and was overwhelmed by culture shock. It was then that I realized just how little I knew about American culture, science, sexuality, and media. I felt unintelligent, different, and confused. In conversations about what was popular, I didn't know what people were talking about or referring to. I asked a lot of questions, which were often met with laughter or perplexed looks from my peers. I looked and sounded American, but I was not American. Everything I knew was foreign to my new peers and I couldn't help but feel that I didn't belong. I looked up a lot of things on the internet to better understand what my peers were talking about. The internet was a relatively new tool to me because we received internet access when I was in tenth grade and the quality of the internet in Papua New Guinea was poor. I had very limited experience with computers and technology. Like everything else in my world, the internet had been monitored and any sites that the organization did not approve of were blocked. At college, I was able to read about and look at ideas, concepts, and pictures that had been off-limits for me. My sheltered world was blown open and I had freedom to explore for the first time in my life. The more I learned and the more I was exposed to about this new culture, the more I realized how much shame, guilt, and confusion I was holding about my body, my sexuality, and my gender.

When I moved to America, I lost my entire sense of safety and community. I was a stranger in a new land, and I had no idea who I was or where I fit. I transferred to four different colleges over a period of five years before graduating with a bachelor of science degree in psychology from a small Christian college in Georgia. I spent my college years trying to find where I belonged. For so many of my peers, college was a time of joy, experimentation, and freedom. For me, it was a time of confusion and growth. My upbringing was far too different from that of my peers and ultimately, I had to focus on finding a sense of safety and belonging in myself. I'll never forget when my mom told me that no matter where I had lived in the world, I had always managed to make each place a home. I now know that just as healing is not a destination, neither is home. The sense of belonging and home comes from within.

As I continued to integrate into this new culture and develop as a woman, I allowed myself to explore and be curious about the things that had always been taboo. I gave myself permission to date and experiment sexually with men and women despite the purity indoctrination I had. I found myself in several physically, emotionally, verbally, and sexually abusive relationships with men during my early 20s. As I look back at those years, I now realize that I had approached dating in a very danger-ous way. Because getting married was such an important part of being a woman in my religious community, I believed that if a man showed interest in me, it was my job to choose him back and to make the relation-ship work. I was told that love was a choice and that you could make any relationship work if you chose to love that person. This message created the belief that if someone was romantically interested in me, I needed to reciprocate that interest regardless of my level of attraction or interest. This resulted in multiple toxic relationships in which I lost much of my self-worth and compromised my core self. Those partners took advan-tage of me emotionally, sexually, and financially. One of these partners was physically abusive and would berate me for hours until I would go completely numb and silent. I lived in constant fear that I would upset this partner, which would result in some form of abuse. This dynamic reinforced my belief that it was my role as a woman to stay quiet and make my male partner(s) happy. I constantly blamed myself for the problems in these relationships because I believed it was my responsibil-ity to make whatever changes needed to be made to make my partner(s) happy. I also believed that I needed a man to lead and protect me. When I look back on the relationships that I had with men, I can now see that they all chose me; I didn't truly take the time to ask myself whether I felt a true connection with or had a desire for them. I was enamored with the idea of what I was told love should look like. Once chosen, I just went along for the ride, changing myself into whatever they wanted me to be to make the relationship work. I didn't give myself the opportunity to get to know these men or take the time to see how I felt about them. My core desire was to be chosen and to be loved. When someone showed inter-est in me, I jumped in with my whole heart. After living through several abusive relationships where I blamed myself for the things that went wrong, I found myself lost and confused about who I was and where I was going. Why hadn't God sent me the husband of my dreams? Was I deserving of love? Would I ever have children? Was the reason I kept getting into unhealthy relationships because God was punishing me for my sins?

At the age of 24, I met the man that I would eventually marry. I thought this man was different from any of the other men I had dated. He appeared to be stable and kind, he was educated, and he wanted to have a family. We dated long distance for two years while I was in graduate school getting my master's degree in social work. After graduation we moved in together, four months before our wedding. I remember the feeling of overwhelming sadness when we first started living together. It was the first time in our relationship where I began to see just how different we were. I spent hours talking to my friends about our relationship and my disappointment. I didn't feel loved the way I had always imagined love would feel. We struggled sexually, which was often blamed on my sexual trauma. I believed it was my job to fix the sexual difficulties we were facing. I often felt that I wasn't intelligent, I wasn't seen, and while my ideas and opinions were listened to, they were not as important or valuable as those of my partner. This relationship mirrored the power dynamics indoctrinated by the church, my community, and purity culture. It was familiar and comfortable because it was all I had ever known. There were two instances early on in our relationship where I told my mother that I didn't think I could stay in the relationship any longer. To my surprise my mother responded with tremendous love and empathy, letting me know that she would support whatever decision I made. Ultimately, I stayed out of fear, obligation, guilt, and hope that it could improve. I was determined to make the relationship work because it was what I had always dreamed of. I was in love with the idea of love and the fairy tale I had been promised. I didn't believe that I could make it on my own without a man to lead and protect me. My greatest desire was to be a mom. I believed that once that happened, I would feel fulfilled and that my fairy tale would be complete. During the 12-year relationship, I gave it all I had. Like anyone, I made many mistakes and was not perfect. Seven years into the marriage I felt hopeless and chose to seek support, love, and attention outside of my marriage from another person. When this relationship came to light, I promised myself that I would do whatever it took to figure out who I was so I could heal. I found an excellent couples therapist who taught us how to communicate effectively and rebuild trust. I worked hard on building my career, caring for my children, and healing my trauma in individual therapy. As I healed and matured, I began to find my voice and learned how to use it. I no longer needed someone to fix me or take care of me. I needed an equal—a partner. Someone who valued me for who I was and not what I could do for them. Someone who wanted to grow alongside me and not control or fix me. Ultimately the marriage did not survive, and we separated. At the time I felt a tremendous sense of failure because I believed that it was my responsibility to keep our relationship and family together no matter what. It was not until months after separating that I realized that the messages I had received about love and marriage as a child had impacted the choices I made in every part of my relationship. The relationship was not based in equality, authenticity, or joy. It was based in compliance, hierarchy, and false promises. It was a perfect replication of everything that had been modeled for me by the religious community I had grown up in.

Near the end of my marriage, I began to unpack the feelings of same-sex attraction that I had buried inside of myself so many years prior. I gave myself permission to answer the hard questions I had been too afraid to ask. Who was I attracted to? What aroused me? What did desire feel like in my body? Who did I feel safe with? With the help of my friends, books, and a few brilliant therapists, I allowed myself to embrace my truth.

A few years before my marriage ended, I began experiencing pain during intercourse. I assumed it was because I had given birth to two children and that my body had changed. I read everything I could find on pain during intercourse and used the tools I had learned while studying to be a sex therapist. I had worked with a significant number of women with similar difficulties and had been able to help them on their journey of healing. Unfortunately, I did not have much success with these tools, so I decided to seek out a pelvic floor physical therapist. In pelvic floor physical therapy, I worked diligently to strengthen my pelvic floor muscles with the hope that my sexual pain would decrease. During one of the internal exams, the pelvic floor physical therapist touched a specific spot in my vagina that sent a shooting pain throughout my entire body. I instantly burst into tears and felt myself leave my body. I dissociated into a childlike state, which in turn triggered my post-traumatic stress disorder. The pelvic floor physical therapist informed me that I was holding a significant amount of trauma in that part of my pelvic floor. I felt so discouraged and broken. I didn't understand what was happening or why this sexual pain had just suddenly shown up one day, so I went to meet with my somatic body therapist. During a session where we spoke to my body, it became very clear that my body no longer desired to have sex with men. The pain I was experiencing during intercourse was my body's way of telling me it wanted it to stop. Tears streamed down my face as I listened to my body. The reality of what it was saying was devastating and yet freeing. My somatic body therapist looked at me with tears in her eyes and said, "Dreya, you have to respect your body and your truth." I knew that I was attracted to and longed to be with a woman. Admitting this in therapy was one thing, but going home and telling my partner, which I thought would result in our marriage falling apart, was something I was too scared to do. With time, I finally found the strength to communicate my feelings and desires, which had a significant impact on our relationship.

I am still navigating this path and continue to work diligently to deconstruct the messages and beliefs that were indoctrinated in me by my religious upbringing about being same-sex attracted. I challenge these messages and beliefs with the hope that I will one day be able to eradicate them and replace them with what I know to be true for me. I know that this is something I will continue to struggle with for a long time, but I am finally in a relationship with someone who loves me for who I am. My wife is patient and understanding of my story and the journey that I am on. She supports my passion for growth and my desire to help create healing in women who have experienced religious trauma. She is the partner I always imagined having and the one I was promised God would reward me with if I obeyed his word and followed his calling. Who knew this partner would ultimately have a vulva and not a penis?

After obtaining a bachelor of science degree in psychology, I pursued my master's degree in social work and decided to pursue the career of becoming a certified sex therapist. During the next few years of school, I found an individual therapist who helped me begin to deconstruct from the belief system I had grown up in, as well as the intense religious sexual shame I had been carrying since childhood. While this journey was extremely painful, it led me to a feeling of freedom and independence that I had never experienced before. The more I learned about sexuality, the more I wanted to learn, leading me to pursue my doctorate in clinical sexology. I knew that I wanted to use my life experiences to help other women who had been controlled and held captive by the beliefs and teachings of the evangelical Christian church and purity culture.

Many of the clients I work with as a therapist in my private practice struggle with their concept of self, pleasure, and sexuality after growing up in evangelical Christian purity culture. Many of these clients live in fear, confusion, and silence about their lack of sexual desire, difficulty with sexual dysfunction, and inability to experience sexual pleasure. It is embarrassing for many of these clients to share that they don't enjoy sex the way they want to. Some of the couples I work with are unable to have penetrative sex or have children due to lack of knowledge, sexual dysfunction, and shame. It is my privilege to walk alongside these clients as they look at the messages they have received and beliefs they have about sex, pleasure, relationships, trauma, and pain. Having grown up in a similar culture to that of my clients, I work hard to meet them where they are and to use the language and framework that they best understand. I focus on a client-centered approach that allows them to lead, since many of them are coming out of or have left unhealthy power dynamics where they were told what to do, think, or feel. I do not want to be another person in their life that allows that dynamic to exist.

When working with clients from highly controlled religious backgrounds, we need to take the time to understand how the client was influenced and what they were taught. Allowing the client to tell their story at their own pace and in their own way gives them autonomy and improves self-esteem. When working with clients from this population, it is not a one-size-fits-all approach. While clients from this population may have grown up indoctrinated with similar values and beliefs, each of them has their own story and ways that they were affected by their indoctrination. When working with these clients I know I need to move slowly and intentionally alongside of them as they work through their emotions and beliefs. I know I cannot show any signs of judgement, or they could potentially shut down and/or end treatment. As I continue to heal myself and gain more knowledge about sexuality, I can help my clients redefine their beliefs around sexuality and ultimately embrace their true sexual selves.

In my doctorate program, I interacted with many other students and professionals in the sex therapy world. One of the themes that began to emerge in the groups and classes I attended was that religion, particularly Christianity, was not discussed in a positive light. As a sex therapist I realized that there was a tremendous need for mental health practitioners and sex therapists who could hold space for clients who were still part of the Christian faith or still held beliefs and values from their evangelical upbringings. Clients who were trying to navigate what they believed and who they wanted to be. Many of these clients were not given accurate or research-based information about sex, pleasure, or consent. It is imperative as a sex therapist to take things slow and use psychosexual education to help these clients build a basic understanding and framework around sexuality. While I no longer associated myself with organized religion or the beliefs of evangelicalism, I have no problem working with clients who do. In fact, I find it extremely fulfilling to help these clients work through their questions, values, and beliefs to redefine what they believe and who they want to be.

As therapists, it is important that we do not let our own biases or beliefs impact the kind of therapy that we provide for our clients. We do not have all the answers, and we need to be willing to think outside of the box, to help our clients. This is what I saw was missing from the classes that I was taking in the field of sex therapy. I took a total of one class on religion and sex, and it did not give me the tools I needed to help these clients. This is when I decided that I wanted to help change that in the field of sex therapy. When it came time for me to write my doctoral dissertation, I chose to create a curriculum for women who had lived through evangelical Christian purity culture. Purity culture created an environment of silence and shame around sexuality in order to isolate and control individuals. I created a curriculum that could be used to bring these women together in a group setting to normalize their experiences, process their beliefs, and help create a support system for them on their healing journey.

It is my hope that in sharing my personal story with you, you can better understand where some of your clients from this population may be coming from. I have also shared parts of my story to decrease the shame and silence around religious trauma, abuse, and effects of purity culture. Shame grows in silence and in darkness. It is my desire to help clients bring their shame into the light to heal and reclaim their sexuality. If you have chosen to read this book, it is my hope that it will allow you to reach your clients in a new and effective way. It is my hope that you leave this book learning something about yourself, and finding ways to help your clients heal. Ultimately, my desire is for every single person in the world to know that they are deserving of pleasure and that their sexuality is unique and beautiful just as it is.

2

✝

Who Is This For?

Evangelical Christianity, with its composition of more than one-fourth of the American population and more than one-third of the American adolescent population, is the largest religious grouping in the United States (Pew Research Center, 2015). Princeton Survey Research Associates International conducted a *Newsweek* poll in 2005 that suggested that 54 percent of American adults identify as born-again or evangelical Christians (Gardner, 2011). This research suggests that that there is likely a significant population that can benefit from the information in this book and through the use of this psychoeducational curriculum. This psychoeducational curriculum was designed for women who grew up in and/or were exposed to the purity messages and programs created by the evangelical Christian church. Because of the intense (and often incorrect) delivery of these messages to participants of the time, many former participants now report difficulties with religious sexual shame, lack of sexual desire, sexual dysfunction, and/or difficulty with constructing a positive body image. Clients who participate in this psychoeducational curriculum will be given the opportunity to identify the messages they received about sex, sexuality, their bodies, pleasure, and their roles as women. Once these messages and beliefs have been identified, the participants will ascertain which of these messages and beliefs they would like to preserve and which they would like to deconstruct and/or discard before reconstructing a new belief system.

"Deconstruction" has recently become somewhat of a buzzword in the world of religion and religious trauma. Deconstruction is a process where an individual looks at and acknowledges how their beliefs, life experiences, and relationships have shaped them and the way they view the world. The focus is on challenging, dissecting, and reviewing the validity and helpfulness of these beliefs in their current life. In the process of deconstruction, the individual attempts to make sense of their emotional, spiritual, and/or sexual beliefs as they process, grieve, and heal. The individual identifies what beliefs they want to keep and what beliefs are no longer in alignment with who they want to be. An important part of deconstruction is encouraging the individual to remain open to their worldview and identity, continuing to fluctuate over the course of their life (Anderson, 2021). Once the individual has worked through deconstruction (although it is never fully complete), the focus turns to the reconstruction of a new religious, spiritual, and/or sexual self. Reconstruction occurs after an individual looks at their prior worldview, beliefs, ideas, and relationships and replaces them with a new foundation that promotes autonomy, authenticity, freedom, self-compassion, and safety (Anderson, 2021). In the process of reconstruction, some individuals choose to leave organized religion altogether, while others choose to embrace a new sense of faith and/or spirituality. Empowerment should be a core focus when working with individuals forging a new path. As providers we want to encourage these individuals to make decisions for themselves. Most highly controlled religious groups do not encourage their members to make decisions for themselves or think for themselves. It is often a culture of strict rules that individuals are expected to follow and not question. In evangelical Christianity, individuals were often taught that the word and the way of God was always right and that they as humans, born sinners, were inherently wrong. In the journey of deconstruction and reconstruction, providers need to encourage the client to own their decisions and invest in the belief that they can create a life and belief system that is aligned with their core values and self.

MENTAL HEALTH PRACTITIONERS

This book and psychoeducational curriculum are intended to be a resource for mental health professionals who want to be better equipped to work with clients who experienced life in evangelical Christianity. Most secular mental health professionals are not specifically trained to work with religious clients despite the large number of psychotherapy clients who have experienced harmful religious indoctrination. This book and curriculum are not anti-God, anti-church, or anti-spirituality, but are anti-dogma. Dogmatic religion is one that does not honor the thoughts or feelings of people. It is one that is static, without room for growth or development (Winell, 1993). The nature of dogmatic religion is to separate from everything else because it claims to have the only truth. Therefore, no matter how altruistic it claims to be, a rigid religion will produce judgment, since there will always be others who believe differently. Judgment will inevitably lead to discrimination and persecution. Dogma does not allow us to come together to understand our shared humanity (Winell, 1993). A dogmatic framework operates on a dualistic basis of right and wrong, reward and punishment. This book and curriculum do not intend to change the religious beliefs of the readers and/or participants. The goal is to create a safe space where individuals can decrease religious sexual shame and navigate how to combine their faith (if the individual maintains their faith) and their sexuality.

As mental health practitioners, it is important for us to remember that an individual's brain cannot unlearn beliefs or concepts. It is our job to help clients identify the origins of their existing neuropathways and help them create new neuropathways. When new neuropathways are created, the old pathways become weaker, and the individual is less likely to go back to their old ways of thinking and maladaptive behaviors (Anderson, 2021). Individuals who grew up in evangelicalism were taught that there is a right and a wrong way to do most things. When helping a client deconstruct and reconstruct their worldview, beliefs, and/or sexual identity, we must emphasize the need for flexibility, space, and uncertainty. There is no right or wrong. It all depends on what the client wants and who they want to be. This may be difficult for these clients to understand because who they were, what they could and could not do, was often dictated by their religion and/or religious community. These individuals rarely had a choice in the matter, which is why giving the client a voice and choice in every step of their journey is pivotal to their healing. Laura Anderson, PhD (2021) states that "true choice involves thought, intention, and curiosity, allowing you to make the decision that is most in line with who you are and what you value" (p. 90).

To provide the best care possible for our clients, it is our responsibility as mental health practitioners to recognize our biases. While this may be briefly discussed in college or grad school, it is something that we need to be more cognizant of when working with clients. Many of us have biases when it comes to faith, religion, and spirituality because we are often affected by this on a personal level. It can be difficult to separate our personal experiences and inherent biases pertaining to religion and/or spirituality from our profession. For this reason, it is imperative that mental health practitioners attend therapy and/or supervision to process their own questions, hangups, and biases.

When working with clients from a religious background, practitioners need to be aware of and understand the importance of providing trauma-informed care. Providers imposing their personal values on clients is the most destructive thing that happens for people who have a negative experience in therapy around religion (Swindle, 2017). As providers, we need to be responsive and not reactive to what the client brings into the room. It is their space, their story, and their healing. It is not about the provider. Paula Swindle states that trauma-informed care is when a care provider has a thorough understanding of the profound neurological, biological, psychological, and social effects of trauma and violence on their client(s). It is the provider's ability to understand the high prevalence of traumatic experiences in someone they are treating therapeutically. Malcolm and Golsworthy's (2019) research found that creating trusting and safe relationships is a vital part of the healing process. We can use the therapeutic relationship that we form with a client to model what safety in nontherapeutic relationships can look like. When working with clients from this population, it is important to ask, "what happened to you" instead of "what's wrong with you." According to the Substance Abuse and Mental Health Services Administration (SAMHSA, n.d.) there are six principles to trauma-informed care. They are:

1. safety;
2. peer support;
3. empowerment, voice, and choice;
4. cultural, historical, and gender issues;
5. trustworthiness and transparency; and
6. collaboration and mutuality.

Creating an environment that focuses on these six principles will allow clients to work through their beliefs, feelings, and experiences in a place that supports curiosity, autonomy, and growth. For many of these women it may be the first time in their lives that they are exposed to such an environment.

SEX THERAPISTS

As a certified sex therapist and a doctor of clinical sexology, I am particularly concerned about the lack of education in the sex therapy field, around how religion can affect sexuality and someone's ability to enjoy sex. While most mental health providers have little to no training on how to work with clients from religious backgrounds, it is even more important for sex therapists to obtain this training. So often, therapists and other mental health providers refer their clients to sex therapists because they do not feel confident or comfortable discussing sex or sexuality. This leaves sex therapists in the position of working in an area of a client's life that other mental health providers often do not wish to explore. Because an individual's sexuality is a significant part of being human, it is extremely important for us to advocate for more education on sexuality in the mental health field. Sexuality is affected by the messages we receive about gender, sex, pleasure, and our bodies. Most often these messages that mold us into who we are as people come from our family, culture, religion, etc. For many individuals, religion is one of the core contributors to how they view sexuality. It is my hope that this book can be used to educate sex therapists on how to help clients from the evangelical Christian population without approaching sexuality from a narrow-minded perspective. It should be noted that there is very little training available for therapists working with evangelical Christians in the sex therapy field. It is imperative that therapists who wish to work with this population have a comprehensive understanding of the culture, religious beliefs, and messages of purity culture. Furthermore, these therapists need to understand the delicate balance of helping a client navigate their sexuality without shame while supporting their client's existing religious beliefs (if they have any). In helping clients reclaim their sexuality and pleasure, practitioners should use therapeutic modalities that allow the client to reprocess and resolve the shame and trauma they have around sexuality. The goal is to create a new sexual ethic, redefine sexuality, and build confidence in their ability to engage in sexuality that feels safe and pleasurable for them (Anderson, 2021, p. 129).

The goal of this book and psychoeducational curriculum is to help foster freedom for the generations of women who have been silenced, controlled, and shamed by the messages of purity culture. In addition, it aims to help these women identify, process, and overcome the sexual difficulties they have experienced by deconstructing false beliefs and utilizing sex therapy tools to educate women about their bodies, pleasure, and sexual ethics. If we as providers can meet the client where they are and hold space for what they believe, while educating them on sexuality from a place of curiosity, research, and patience, I believe that we will see much better results in their treatment. The ultimate goal for clients is sexual healing. Sexual healing is achieved when an individual can embrace pleasure and authentic sexual expression in ways that feel both internally and externally safe (Anderson, 2021, p. 142).

Looking for a therapist is difficult on its own, let alone looking for a sex therapist, let alone looking for a sex therapist versed in religious sexual trauma. It is especially difficult when a client comes from a conservative background where they were told that sex is only for people who are married and that it should not be discussed with anyone outside of the church. Women who grew up in evangelical Christianity were often told that they would be rewarded with amazing sex if they waited to have sex until they got married. They did not receive education about what arousal could look like or feel like in their bodies. In purity culture, the body and sexuality were often viewed as one and the same, and women were told they could not trust themselves or their bodies. Many women learned to dissociate or disconnect from their bodies entirely because the body was the avenue to sex and sexuality. Being in their bodies and allowing themselves to feel was dangerous, which resulted in many of these women disconnecting from their body to remain pure. The problem with that, despite what the church promised, is that there is no light switch you can flip to go from disconnection from body and sexuality to connection. Many of these women were not educated about sexual development and were taught to ignore or avoid anything related to arousal, desire, or sexuality. This meant that when they found themselves married and in a position where they were allowed to access these parts of themselves, they responded in a similar way to individuals who have been sexually assaulted. Some of the physiological responses were anorgasmia, disgust around or avoidance of sex, vaginismus, vulvodynia, shame, guilt, anxiety, and complete shutdown. There is a significant need for sex therapists to understand the culture that these women come from to provide the support, psychosexual education, and therapy that they so desperately need.

BENEFITS TO PARTICIPANTS

I have worked with many women who grew up in and/or were exposed to the teachings of evangelical Christian purity culture. Many of these women have carried guilt and sexual shame into adulthood, directly impacting their relationships. Some of the sexual difficulties and/or dysfunctions sex therapists have identified when working with this population include low libido, anxiety during sexual activity, vaginal pain disorders, dissociation during sexual activity, fear around talking about sex or anything pertaining to sexuality, inability to experience sexual pleasure and/or orgasm, and general disgust for and/or avoidance of sex. When working with these women, it is important to always begin a session by asking them what messages they received from purity culture about sex, their body, marriage, and pleasure. Finch (2019) observes, "The normal desires for intimacy, connection, pleasure, and sensuality, were painted as dark, evil, and dirty" (p. 55). Most often, these women state that they received very limited information about their bodies, sexuality, masturbation, or pleasure. Instead of this pertinent information, they received curriculum and instruction focused on modesty for women, fear tactics, subservience to men (in some cases), and unwavering protection of their virgin status until marriage. In a fascinating distortion of the truth, these women were trained as adolescents to feel directly responsible for protecting men from sexual sin. Women were referred to as the "gatekeepers" to sex. Upon marriage, these same women were expected to drop all pretenses of modesty and become sexual goddesses who were wholeheartedly sexually submissive to their husbands. Linda Kay Klein (2018) states that the purity movement teaches us that a "pure" woman comes to her husband an untouched virgin who has hardly (if ever) thought about sex before. And then, naturally and beautifully, the woman's new husband introduces his wife to sexuality for the first time, and years of pent-up sexual energy, which she was not even aware of, comes pouring out of her, allowing her to meet her new husband's every sexual want, which is also her every want, and together they live happily ever after (p. 137). These women were told that if they waited to have sex until they got married, they would be blessed with amazing sex lives. A poll conducted by Sheila Wray Gregoire and colleagues (2021) found that only 52 percent of the women who remained virgins until their wedding night (due to religious teachings) were aroused the first time they had sex. Women were not taught that sexual activity requires both partners to give and take in equal amounts, or that sex is created to be pleasurable, and all parties involved should participate fully and consent to all activity. They were not taught that sex for pleasure is not a sin and that sex without the goal of conception is acceptable. Nowhere was it discussed that sex is a journey that can often take a lifetime to understand. These women were not taught about the importance of pleasure, both giving and receiving. Through the countless lessons, events, pledges, videos, and books, the topic of female sexual pleasure was either ignored, buried, devalued, or outright shamed.

In an effort to help these women find a healthy, safe, and fulfilling sexual lifestyle, this book and psychoeducational curriculum is designed to counter the messages of purity culture and fill in the missing gaps of instruction in female anatomy, sexual pleasure, and female sexual health. One might be surprised to learn that many of the women who grew up in evangelical Christian purity culture have never even looked at their vulvas, are afraid to touch themselves or masturbate, and have even reported never having experienced an orgasm alone and/or with a partner. Addressing sexual anatomy will be one of the first topics addressed in the psychoeducational curriculum. Using pictures and diagrams of female anatomy to provide a basis for further discussion of sex is a crucial first step. Selections from resources such as *Come as You Are* (2015a) by Emily Nagoski, *Becoming Cliterate* (2017) by Laurie Mintz, and the online video library from the website OMG Yes, will be used to educate participants about masturbation, self-discovery, and sexual pleasure. Once the participants have a better understanding of their own sexual anatomy and how to derive personal sexual pleasure, we will also (optionally) discuss how to incorporate a partner or partners. In purity culture, if there is any actual instruction on sexual intercourse, the focus is typically on penile and vaginal intercourse, procreation, and the sexual satisfaction of men. Routinely, sex therapists find these female clients who were exposed to purity culture report low desire, sexual avoidance, anxiety around sex, and the feeling that sex is a "chore." In these final stages of rewriting the internalized sexual narrative, the psychoeducational curriculum will focus on helping participants create sexual ethics and teach them how to communicate their sexual desires and needs to their partner(s). Much of the psychoeducational curriculum focuses on the work of Dianna Anderson. Anderson (2015) describes the six ways of defining sexual ethics for women who grew up in purity culture:

1. Sexuality has many facets.
2. Your body is your own. You are not public property.
3. Healthy sexuality requires understanding your own body.
4. Sexual activity should always be pleasurable and consensual.
5. Sexuality is fluid and complex.
6. God doesn't shame us (p. 54).

Other goals would be maintaining openness, identifying opportunities for mutual pleasure, teaching them a language around sex, and letting participants know that they truly deserve to and can enjoy sex.

HOW TO USE THIS CURRICULUM

This psychoeducational curriculum is designed to be used in a small group setting of six to eight participants. Small group settings tend to produce more intimacy than larger groups and are likely to result in more member participation (Corey, 2011; Garvin, 1996). Upon review of the curriculum and the time constraints of 90-minute sessions, it became apparent that there would be insufficient time and/or resources to process the individual thoughts and experiences of each individual participant. Therefore, a psychoeducational group format was chosen versus a processing group. A psychoeducational group is one where participants focus on thinking about and creating new skills or ideas about a specific topic. Psychoeducational groups can help normalize the issues that the participants have often felt they were alone in experiencing. In psychoeducational groups, participants often obtain a sense of belonging and community. Since the topic of sexuality was often not discussed in evangelical Christian circles, it left many of its members feeling confused and alone in their questions and experiences. The intent of using this curriculum in a group setting is to create a sense of camaraderie between the participants, normalizing their experiences, questions, and desires so that they no longer feel alone.

Deconstructing or challenging one's core beliefs can impact an individual's entire family system. In an effort to address the additional therapeutic processing needs of participants, participants should be required to demonstrate that they are actively attending individual or couples therapy with a licensed mental health professional. This requirement is intended to assist participants with processing any emotional conflicts or difficulties that may arise given the nature of the curriculum's subject matter. In addition to the requirement to participate in individual/couples therapy, participants should be required to complete an informed consent document. The informed consent will follow the requirements of the American Counseling Association Code of Ethics (2014). The informed consent will include the purpose and goals of the psychoeducational group and curriculum, the techniques and tools used, possible limitations and/or risks of the curricula, and expected benefits. Informed consent should be given to participants prior to the first class and then reviewed orally at the beginning of the first class.

3

✝

History of Evangelicalism and Purity Culture

The story of American evangelicalism has roots in early British Protestant reforms dating back to the eighteenth century. Protestant sects (the main branches of the Reformation) believed that humanity was at war with sin and temptation. They believed that all people were born sinful and could obtain salvation through following the teachings of the Bible. These religious sects, who later became known as evangelicals, encouraged their members to abstain from sin and temptation (Hart, 2002). Some of the distinguishing characteristics of evangelicals are their belief in the historical accuracy and literal interpretation of the Bible, particularly the divinity, death, and resurrection of Jesus Christ, and the need for personal conversion or being "born again" to obtain salvation (Finch, 2019). Evangelicals held revival events that focused on preaching in a way "designed to bring hearers to a point of crisis, at which they despaired over their sinfulness and experienced the love of God in an immediate way" (Hart, 2002, p. 7). Once a community or individual professed to be "born again," the focus turned to "holy living," which was defined by "behaving in a visibly devout manner, whether by abstaining from certain worldly activities or by performing righteous deeds" (Hart, 2002, p. 7). While each denomination went through a variety of reforms over the following two centuries, it is important to note that they remained separate entities rather than combining as one evangelical church.

American evangelicalism is now described as a movement focused on "witnessing the gospel." Author Douglas Sweeney (2005) describes evangelicals as a combination of Christian believers that also happen to be members of various Protestant denominations including, but not limited to, Anglicans, Methodists, Pentecostals, Lutherans, and Anabaptist evangelicals, among others. Sweeney (2005) admits, "we have no card-carrying membership, not even an official membership list" (p. 20). In *Evangelicalism and the Future of Christianity* (1996), Alister McGrath states that evangelicals subscribe to six core convictions, which are a belief in God; a belief in Jesus Christ as the savior of humanity; a belief in the existence of the Holy Spirit; the need for a personal conversion experience; the need for evangelism (preaching the gospel) to the world; and a belief in the importance of the Christian community for fellowship and spiritual growth. These core convictions helped the various denominations unite a movement around topics such as purity to stand up against the sins and immorality of society. According to Anderson (2015), "Sexual purity has become the one means by which the Evangelical Church separates itself from the world" (p. 20). Joe Carter of the Gospel Coalition describes the Purity Culture movement as a product of the 1980s–1990s attempts to address pressing sexual topics like the AIDS epidemic, all-time high teen pregnancy rates, and a dramatic increase in premarital sex rates. At the core of the promotion of sexual abstinence is the evangelical Christian church, but sexual abstinence is not just about sex; it is connected to morals, religion, and politics (Gardner, 2011).

The Adolescent Family Life Act (AFLA) was signed into law by President Ronald Reagan in 1981 (Colvin, 2020). Senator Jeremiah Denton and Senator Orrin Hatch created the AFLA in the hopes that it would address teen pregnancy. Denton and Hatch wanted the federal government to mandate and promote "chastity and self-discipline" programs for teenagers (AFLA, as cited in Saul, 1998, para. 7). The AFLA's initial grants were used by religious groups to create curricula such as Sex Respect and the Silver Ring Thing. Initially heralded as a "down-to-earth program designed to provide teens with information" (Sex Respect Student Workbook, 2019), Sex Respect was filled with racial and homophobic bias, gender stereotyping, and fear tactics trying to convince teens to say "no" to sex (Rethinking Schools, 2020).

President George W. Bush was an advocate for government funding of abstinence education, and in 1996 the Welfare Reform Act was passed. $1.5 billion in federal funding was put into abstinence-only education in hopes that it would help reduce teen pregnancy and abortion rates. Between 1991 and 2005 teen pregnancy rates dropped by 34 percent and teen abortion rates dropped 39 percent between 1990 and 1999. While abstinence supporters gave credit for these changes to abstinence-only education, a study conducted in 2009 by the Centers for Disease Control and Prevention (CDC) found that teenage pregnancy rates increased by 3 percent in 2006. In 2010 President Barack Obama cut funding for abstinence-only programs and put funding into comprehensive sex education instead (Gardner, 2011). Comprehensive sex education advocates criticize abstinence-only education because they believe it is more about religion and morality than it is about healthy sex education.

The American evangelical sexual abstinence campaigns began in the early 1990s in reaction to what the evangelical church felt was a hypersexualized culture. Defining society as hypersexual allowed evangelicals to identify as a minority, which allowed them to reclaim power and motivate a generation of followers to make what they felt were the right choices about sex and their bodies (Gardner, 2011). The evangelical church believed that the American culture was normalizing teenage sexual activity and insinuating that its youth had no choice when it came to having sex. The president of Southern Baptist Theological Seminary, Albert Mohler, stated that debating whether sexual abstinence before marriage was realistic or not should not be the focus. Instead, Mohler stated that sexual abstinence was a biblical command and therefore a realistic expectation that should be upheld by parents and their teenagers (Gardner, 2011). Evangelical sexual abstinence campaigns argued that delaying sexual gratification before marriage would be rewarded with true love and amazing sex in marriage. For evangelicals, sex was only acceptable within the context of heterosexual marriage, making marriage not only the goal, but also implying that a good marriage with fulfilling sex, void of emotional baggage, would be the reward for those who were sexually abstinent. Thus, the goal of abstinence became marriage and great sex, which transformed the message of "abstain from sex" to a more positive message of "wait for sex" (Gardner, 2011). This belief was reinforced with youth, using the fairy-tale narrative. Young women were referred to as princesses waiting for their prince to come sweep them off their feet. They were told to focus on modesty and purity in order to protect themselves and their future prince. Young men were encouraged to pursue and protect their princess and her virtue at all costs. This fairy-tale narrative was used in many of the books written on marriage, sex, and dating by Christian authors of the time.

The True Love Waits organization was founded in 1993 by Jimmy Hester and Richard Ross and is often credited with launching the evangelical sexual abstinence movement (Gardner, 2011). The idea for True Love Waits came from a Christian sex education project that Hester and Ross collaborated on while working at Lifeway, a Christian publisher, in 1987. True Love Waits was known for holding large youth rallies that included evangelism, testimonies about abstinence, and Christian musical artists. At these True Love Waits rallies, attendees were encouraged to sign an abstinence pledge card that read: "Believing that true love waits, I make a commitment to God, myself, my family, my friends, my future mate, and my future children to be sexually abstinent from this day until the day I enter a biblical marriage relationship" (Gardner, 2011, p. 7). The first national display of signed pledge cards to abstain from premarital sex took place at the National Mall in 2004 where 210,000 cards were signed by over 25,000 attendants (Gardner, 2011). Rings that read True Love Waits, became very popular among Christian youth who wanted to pledge abstinence and purity until marriage. The purity ring represented the gift of virginity and the commitment to preserve this gift until one's wedding day. Purity rings demonstrated the wearers' ability to control their sexuality and give it away at the time of marriage (Gardner, 2011). Although many teenagers signed pledge cards committing to abstain from sex until marriage, this does not mean that they were not engaging in sexual activity. This is because the focus of these campaigns was on not having sex, but they rarely defined what other activities to avoid, leaving these individuals to navigate their sexuality on their own (Gardner, 2011). Over the course of the next few years, rallies, media events, and conventions took place in the United States promoting the campaign. Churches and publishers noticed the success of the True Love Waits campaign and began to create curricula, media, family events, and memorabilia to support the movement. With state school systems investing in and promoting abstinence-only sex education programs (using abundant federal funds thanks to the AFLA), American Evangelical churches sought to reinforce the lessons taught while promoting additional non-secular themes to their congregants. These themes included an additional focus on the importance of virginity until marriage, avoiding sexual temptations, and women being responsible for protecting men from sexual sin. These themes were reinforced through curriculum materials, pledges, events such as purity balls, and even purity rings designed to remind the wearer to remain pure (Rosenbloom, 2005). While True Love Waits no longer holds events in large arenas, it still offers curricula, devotional guides, and jewelry that churches and youth leaders can purchase and use at private events (Gardner, 2011).

Pure Freedom was founded in 1996 by former marketing consultant, Dannah Gresh, whose goal was to educate young girls about how to live a sexually pure life. The mission of Pure Freedom was to "equip men and women of all ages to live a vibrant life of purity, to experience healing from past impurity if it exists in their lives and to experience a vibrant passionate marriage which portrays the love Christ has for his Bride the church" (Gardner, 2011, p. 9). Most abstinence groups focused on the negative consequences of premarital sex in the materials given to participants as well as the messages shared at events that they held. Pure Freedom made a distinction between "poor choices," and "wise choices." A poor choice was the choice to engage in premarital sex, which was not in alignment with God's design. Pure Freedom taught its participants that some of the negative consequences they may experience included emotional stress, unwanted pregnancy, and sexually transmitted infections (STIs)(Gardner, 2011).

Another well-known organization, Silver Ring Thing, was created by Denny and Amy Pattyn in 1996. Silver Ring Thing was created in response to their belief that teen pregnancy was on the rise and that promoting abstinence outside of marriage was the only way to fix this. Programs put on by Silver Ring Thing have been described as "part rave, part Saturday Night Live, and part Saturday night revival" (Gardner, 2011, p. 8). While abstinence was a major focus of these organizations, purity was another key focus. Abstinence was a conscious choice to not engage in a specific behavior, while the concept of purity extended as part of someone's identity. Purity was a way of life or a lifestyle choice—one where an individual was intentional about what they wore, the way they conducted themselves, what they watched or listened to, what they allowed themselves to think about, and what they said. The Silver Ring Thing study Bible stated, "purity is not about what you cannot do but rather about treasuring who you are" (Gardner, 2011, pp. 29–30). The shift in focus from abstinence to purity allowed evangelical abstinence groups the freedom to avoid explicitly defining acceptable versus unacceptable sexual behavior. Instead, the groups were able to focus on the choice of living a pure lifestyle that included waiting for true love and marriage before having sex. Silver Ring Thing is the only evangelical abstinence organization that received federal funding for its abstinence education. Silver Ring Thing received over $1 million in government money between 2003 and 2006 (Gardner, 2011).

By 2003, abstinence-only education was used in the majority of public schools. While there was language in various federal funding bills to not directly support religious or faith-based lessons, the hunger for abstinence-only curricula led to a lack of oversight coupled with a willingness from Christian publishers to take whatever funding came their way (Anderson, 2015). While these initial abstinence-only and purity programs were heralded as successes (a 2009 CDC study noted a significant decline of sexual activity for girls ages 15 to 17 and boys ages 15 to 18; Carter, 2019), additional evidence from a study completed in 2009 found that the actual sexual behaviors of teens who took purity pledges did not differ dramatically from the sexual behaviors of teens that did not. A study by the National Longitudinal Study of Adolescent Health found that individuals who signed abstinence pledges only delayed sexual debut by 18 months (Gardner, 2011). In addition, another study found the rates of STIs did not statistically differ between pledge and non-pledge individuals (Carter, 2019).

Anderson (2015) argues that while the purity movement may have had good intentions, it has resulted in a destructive path of misogyny and exclusion. Without a doubt, multiple generations have felt the impact of this movement on their sexual beliefs and experiences. Mental health practitioners and sex therapists have an opportunity to help those affected by this well-intentioned, but sex-negative and ultimately destructive culture. This book and psychoeducational curriculum are intended as a valuable tool for individuals and therapists trying to address the psychological and sexual impact experienced by women exposed to purity culture.

4

✛

Women in Purity Culture

Women in the evangelical Christian church during the 1980s through the early 2000s were exposed to sex-negative messages that were developed by the church as a response to the changing sexual climate and their fear of losing the traditional family. Evangelical Christians "were concerned with domestic life and the proper execution of the roles of men and women as husbands and wives within the nuclear family" (Fitzgerald, 2017, p. 196). The messages and focus of the evangelical Christian church during this time are now referred to as purity culture. Evangelical Christians are specifically credited with developing a purity culture movement that sought to address perceived cultural threats, including increasing teen pregnancy rates, the AIDS epidemic, sexually transmitted infections (STIs), and an alleged moral decline in youth. The movement is often attributed to evangelical fears that they would lose the sanctity of marriage after witnessing the sexual revolution of the 1960s. The so-called separation of church and state was a guiding national principle in politics and religious matters in the late nineteenth and early twentieth centuries. The evangelical Christian church, in an attempt to address these cultural threats, began disassembling that wall through their political activism, lobbying, and the creation of a steady supply of public-school abstinence-only curricula. In addition to these activities, they further sought to reinforce these beliefs in churches, youth groups, Christian schools, and religious communities. While the underlying precepts of abstinence-only education in society have not changed significantly in centuries, the development of far-reaching curricula, workshops, books, classroom materials, abstinence pledges, and even purity merchandise has brought about a far more systematic method of delivery for church doctrine.

The purity culture movement may have had good intentions, but ultimately it became destructive for many. Unfortunately, that destruction was predominantly shouldered by women, leaving a generation of Christian women struggling with unrealistic expectations, disappointment, hurt, sexual dysfunction, and sexual shame (Anderson, 2015). For adolescent girls who grew up in purity culture, messages of modesty, purity, and the importance of remaining a virgin until marriage were pervasive. Modesty was presented as a form of influence and control that women had over men. Dressing modestly allowed women to guard and protect the men in their community from lustful, therefore sinful, thoughts or actions. Teenage girls were taught that all men, including the fathers of their friends, would struggle with lusting after them. Attraction was equated with lust, which turned the focus on the bodies of women. Men either avoided women and their bodies or lusted after their bodies. The teachings of purity culture put the responsibility for the behaviors of men on the shoulders of adolescent girls (Gregoire et al., 2021). Women were taught that their husband would be intoxicated by their body. By dressing immodestly, they would arouse and tempt other men, which was sinful. Many women believed that their bodies were dangerous because they had the ability to affect and/or damage the spiritual lives of men. In *Damaged Goods* (2015), Dianna Anderson states that purity proponents believe that sex is a physical, emotional, and spiritually binding act in a heterosexual marriage. In addition, purity means not having sexual or lustful thoughts, that men and women belong to their spouses, and above all, premarital sex is a sin.

Materials from this time were especially focused on the preservation of virginity. Jessica Valenti, the author of *The Purity Myth* (2010), explains that "people have been talking authoritatively about virginity for thousands of years, yet we don't even have a working medical definition for it" (p. 20). While there is no working medical definition for virginity, purity culture often defines virginity as the lack of penile and vaginal penetration. Another aspect of virginity in purity culture is emotional purity, which is the belief that one can become impure by becoming emotionally involved with the opposite sex, even if physical contact doesn't take place (Anderson, 2015). Girls were routinely taught that their greatest gifts (and what gave them value as Christian women) were their bodies and their "intact" virginity. Anderson (2015) states that purity teachings implied that sexual abstinence outside of marriage was a way for adolescents to live out their faith. Sara Moslener, historian and author of *Virgin Nation: Sexual Purity and American Adolescence* (2015), notes that James Dobson, a Christian evangelical author and founder of the conservative Focus on the

Family ministry, described "female sexuality as a commodity that reaches the height of its value on the wedding day" (p. 103).

For individuals who had already had sex, the evangelical Christian church offered a second virginity or renewed virginity. Abstinence groups like True Love Waits, Silver Ring Thing, and Pure Freedom all offered the option of a second virginity as a choice for individuals who chose to repent and then rededicate themselves to abstaining from sex until heterosexual marriage (Gardner, 2011). This concept enhanced the agency of individuals and reiterated their ability to lose, find, take, and give their virginity. While renewed virginity was encouraged and acceptable, it was not as highly valued as first-time virginity because the gift of virginity to one's spouse was something highly prized (Gardner, 2011).

In addition to a focus on virginity, girls subjected to purity culture were heavily dissuaded from exploring sexual pleasure and/or their bodies. Girls were often told not to trust themselves or their bodies because their true nature was corrupted by sin. The female body was the root of evil and had caused the initial fall of man (Finch, 2019). These girls were not given a language for sex or sexuality and were ultimately promised incredible sex lives once they got married so long as they remained "pure" before marriage. Jamie Lee Finch (2019) states that "the majority of what comes out of the religious rhetoric is wrapped up in language that describes the physical body, the root of all that is evil, or 'sinful.' Natural human desires are described as ungodly and dangerous, and are required to be suppressed until (implied heterosexual) marriage in order to be holy" (Finch, 2019, p. 31). These messages deeply affected the sexual development, beliefs, and experiences of women for decades to come. According to Ingersoll (2003), traditional evangelicals prided themselves on laying out a clear, concrete, unchanging blueprint for gender distinctions. They believed that wives should submit to their husbands, who lovingly lead their families; that pastoral authority and church leadership roles were prohibited to women; and that, when possible, women should find their callings at home caring for their families. They ground this perspective in the variety of biblical texts and in the historical teachings of Christianity, which they believed require the subordination of women to men. (p. 17)

Tina Sellers, author of *Sex, God, and the Conservative Church* (2017), notes that women were promised a happily ever after if they were willing to abstain from sex until marriage, chose a Christian husband, and raised their children in the church. Unfortunately, they often found that the results of following these rules routinely fell short of their expectations. In addition to inhabiting marriages that did not meet their expectations, they were often left with immense shame that affected their sexual selves for years to come. Prominent purity culture author Dianna Anderson (2015) writes that the influence of the consistent shaming embedded in the religious purity message, particularly during stages of extreme neural plasticity, such as adolescence, can significantly impact sexual development. After all, researchers have found that our brains bend toward whatever it is that our attention is directed to. If an adolescent is regularly exposed to shaming messages—like the message that a girl or woman is utterly and fundamentally pure or impure, good or bad, pleasing or displeasing, desirable or undesirable, et cetera, based on her sexual expressions or lack thereof—she will become more likely to experience shame in association with sex than she otherwise may have been (p. 14).

The deployment of this modern purity culture has, without a doubt, had long-lasting negative sexual and psychological effects on many of its participants. Beale et al. (2016) found that women in purity culture report significantly higher levels of guilt around sex. In addition, strongly religious women in their study reported greater rates of unsatisfactory sex, higher anxiety levels about that sex, and a prevailing feeling of being incapable of changing their situation. Anderson (2015) states that evangelical adolescents are less likely to expect sex to be pleasurable and are more likely to expect that having sex will result in feeling guilty.

5

+

Shame

Shame is not a new topic to researchers. Well-known researcher Brené Brown (2021) brilliantly defines shame as "the intensely painful feeling or experience of believing that we are flawed and therefore unworthy of love, belonging, and connection" (p. 37). Rosemary Mills (2004), studying shame in young girls, once defined shame as "blaming the self in its entirety" (p. 30). While shame is well researched and supported by various scientific measures, researchers admit that research on sexual shame is lacking. In fact, much research on sexual shame has occurred only in the past twenty years. Ironically, researchers steered clear of sexual shame research and measures due to the perceived taboo status of sexual shame. Jeffrey Weeks (1989) stated that "the erotic still arouses acute moral anxiety and confusion. This is not because sex is intrinsically 'naughty,' but because it is a focus for powerful feelings" (p. 18). Sex brings up emotion(s) when it is discussed, which can make it a difficult topic to research because the researchers involved could most definitely show bias based on their life experiences and/or beliefs. Using Brené Brown's definition of shame as the basis for creating a definition of sexual shame, one could define sexual shame as an intensely painful feeling or experience resulting in the belief that we are flawed and therefore unworthy of acceptance and belonging due to our sexual thoughts, experiences, or behaviors. Individuals are often very young when they are introduced to sexual shame, whether through sexual secrecy, sexual abuse, exposure to pornography, religious shaming, being dressed to hide the body, or being shamed for masturbation or promiscuity (Hastings, 1998).

A subcategory of sexual shame is religious sexual shame. Several research studies have demonstrated a link between sex guilt, sexual behavior, sexual attitudes, and religiosity (McClintock, 2001; Tangney & Dearing, 2003). It's hard to research shame and sexual shame without running across religion and the effects it has had on the feelings, beliefs, and shame individuals carry with them throughout life. Shaming is often common in religious communities because it is intertwined in the core beliefs, theology, and doctrine, which can make it difficult to see (Anderson, 2015). Women, in particular, have carried around religious sexual shame for centuries due to the teachings of many religions. Reporting the results of a study by Fox and Young (1989), and Anderson (2015) notes that girls are 92 percent more likely to experience sexual guilt than boys (p. 27).

In the evangelical Christian community, women have been viewed as the gatekeepers to sexuality. Women are told that they are less sexual than men and are therefore the gatekeepers of sexual morals within the community (Anderson, 2015). While there is no research proving this, these women grow up in a world where they often feel shame about their bodies, their sexual desire, and all things sex-related. They aren't taught to ask why God might have given them their desires for sexual intimacy, why God invented sex, or even why men and women are wired differently as sexual creatures (Sellers, 2017). When sexuality is discussed in church settings, the conversation is often focused on the concept of purity, especially when it comes to women (Beck, 2006). Anderson (2015) states that in the evangelical community, an "impure" girl or woman isn't just seen as damaged; she's considered dangerous. She is dangerous to the men and the community because if the heads of the male leaders fall, everything in the community will crumble. Women feel the pressure to remain pure and virginal in order to give themselves value while also feeling responsible to keep men pure. The purity movement addressed lust and modesty in such a way that women were made to feel responsible for how men behaved. Women were expected to wear modest clothing to keep men from "stumbling." This taught women to distrust men and taught men that they were not responsible for their behavior or sexual desires. This encouraged women to view their own sexual desires and bodies as dangerous, causing many of them to bury or hide their sexual feelings (Sellers, 2017). Some evangelicals find themselves unable to express their sexuality when they do get married because they struggle to see it as a good, God-given gift, after so many years of shaming themselves for having natural erotic thoughts and feelings (Sellers, 2017). These completely healthy and natural feelings and/or desires that are part of the human experience are painted in a light that insinuates they are unnatural or bad. Women are left feeling confused and alone in their experiences.

The evangelical church often creates an environment that encourages silence around sex, making it even harder for women to communicate their feelings and questions when it comes to sex and sexuality. Sellers (2017) has found in her research that around 80 percent of people raised in the United States grew up in homes that were silent, ignorant, or reactive about sexuality and sexual development (p. 105). It is not a far reach to assume that this percentage would be even higher in religious homes. Paul Gilbert (2003) explored the differences between internal versus external shame, where external is concerned with the evaluation of others, while internal is related to internal self-judgment. Gilbert notes that internal shame goes past self-criticism and enters an area of hostility toward the self. When these women feel hostility toward themselves, they often feel powerless or worthless, which in turn makes them seclude themselves from others and push others away. Conklin (2019) states that "when an internal shame reaction is deeply embedded within a person, self-compassion is a stark deviation from one's natural response" (p. 3).

There is also a positive link between sexual shame and alienation from God, indicating that individuals experiencing sexual shame may believe that God has abandoned or punished them for their actions or thoughts (Marcinechová & Záhorcová, 2020). Sellers (2017) states that when working with Christian clients who have experienced religious sexual shame it is imperative that we help them "see their belovedness and begin to live into a sex-positive Gospel ethic, one in which they feel seen, known, loved, and accepted while they seek to see, know, love, and accept another" (p. 99). Helping these women identify and process the shame they have carried from exposure to religious teachings and beliefs is imperative because certain religious beliefs can stifle sexual expression to the point that individuals incur significant emotional distress (Murray et al., 2007).

Moving from a sex-negative framework to a sex-positive one will enable these women to experience healthy and pleasurable sex. Helping these women combine new sexual ethics and beliefs with their faith can be life changing. Anderson (2015) describes healthy sexuality as one that "takes others into account, that asks for maturity and understanding and respects others and their bodies. . . . It does not place sex on a pedestal, allowing it to overpower a person's life, or let it take unnecessary precedence over one's spiritual life" (p. 40). Religious sexual shame affects many areas of a woman's life. Helping these women identify and deconstruct this shame and replace it with confidence in themselves as women and as sexual beings has the potential to change not only their lives but also the entire culture moving forward. This newfound freedom, through information, education, and empowerment, will potentially lead to improvements in self-confidence, embracing one's sexuality, experiencing

pleasure, and ultimately finding sexual satisfaction. One remains hope-
ful that the participants will, in part, likely educate their own children,
friends, and family members about these concepts, ultimately resulting
in the change from a sex-negative culture to a sex-positive one. Mental
health practitioners and sex therapists will benefit from learning how
to reach this population and help them embrace pleasure and sexuality.

6

✢

Sexual Dysfunction

According to a study conducted by *BMC Women's Health* in 2018, about 41 percent of reproductive-aged women experience some form of sexual dysfunction (McCool-Myers et al., 2018). The *Diagnostic and Statistical Manual of Mental Disorders* (APA, 2013) states that female sexual dysfunction consists of sexual interest/arousal disorder, female orgasmic disorder, and genito-pelvic pain/penetration disorder. When looking at female sexual dysfunction, we want to approach it from a biopsychosocial perspective. Female sexual dysfunction is impacted by an individual's biological, psychological, and social experiences. West et al.'s 2004 systematic review of female sexual dysfunction found that physical health, psychological health, race/ethnicity, number of sexual partners, religion, sexual orientation, communication, and attitudes toward sex can all impact sexual dysfunction (West et al., 2004). Significant risk factors that are consistent in female sexual dysfunction are poor physical health, poor mental health, poor partner health, unemployment of a partner, low education of a partner, stress, abortion, menopause, genitourinary problems, female genital mutilation, relationship dissatisfaction, sexual dysfunction of a partner, sexual abuse, and being religious (McCool-Myers et al., 2018). Sexual dysfunction can prevent an individual from desiring, having, or enjoying sex. Sexual pain can often increase low self-esteem because many women feel that there is something wrong with them or that they are unable to meet the sexual expectations or desires of their partner(s). The fear of experiencing pain during sex can turn into hypervigilance, anxiety, or depression, which can in turn create a feeling of disconnection (Coady & Fish, 2011).

In my work as a certified sex therapist, I have found that sexual dysfunction is common among women who grew up in evangelical purity culture, which aligns with Simpson and Ramberg (1992), who found a significant link between people who had highly religious upbringings and sexual dysfunction. Another study found that women who felt guilt about experiencing sexual pleasure were more likely to experience sexual dysfunction (Woo, 2001). The most common forms of sexual dysfunction that I have come across in my work with evangelical women are lack of sexual desire/low libido, avoidance of or aversion to sex, pain during or after sex, and anorgasmia. When women come seeking help for low libido or lack of sexual desire, it is important to reassure them that there is nothing wrong with their libido or desire. There is an assumption in our culture that having a higher libido is better than having a lower libido. I encourage my clients to focus on embracing the libido that they have just as it is. Instead of shaming themselves for not having a higher libido, I encourage them to focus on learning about and understanding the libido they have. Women who struggle with a lack of sexual desire often blame themselves or feel that there is something wrong with them. I have found that one of the core reasons many of these women have a decreased interest in sex or pleasure is that they are not having the kind of sex that they desire. Often, these women are focused on giving their partners pleasure and are not focused on experiencing or receiving pleasure themselves.

Many of the Christian books written about sex and marriage promote a hierarchical view of marriage, in which the husband is the primary decision-maker and the wife is the follower. A well-known book in the evangelical world, *Love & Respect* (Eggerichs, 2004) states that marriages that consist of two equals are destined to fail because there needs to be someone who is in charge. The author states that one of the reasons divorce is so prevalent in our society is that we have been promoting a relationship style in which is there are two equals (Gregoire et al., 2021). Sheila Wray Gregoire and colleagues (2021) state that couples who embraced hierarchy are 7.4 percent more likely to get a divorce compared to couples who share decision-making power. Marriages in which women do not feel heard, and where their opinions are less important than those of their husband are 26 percent more likely to end in divorce (Gregoire et al., 2021). This is congruent with research conducted by the Gottman Institute, which found that marriages in which a man is unwilling to share power with his partner are 81 percent more likely to end in divorce (Gregoire et al., 2021). This hierarchical template for marriage is not only valued by evangelicals, but is also valued in sex. An online poll conducted on Twitter and Facebook with 1,500 participants found that 95 percent of the respondents felt the message about sex in the evangelical church focused on the fulfillment of the husband, while ignoring that of the wife (Gregoire et al., 2021).

In my work with clients, I ask them to identify what motivates them to pursue sex or intimacy. I have them identify what they want to feel when they have sex and what sorts of touch and/or pleasure they desire. Lastly, I have them describe in detail what sex worth having would look like, taste like, feel like, sound like, and smell like for them. For many of these clients, this is the first time they have given themselves permission to even think about what they want or what gives them pleasure. More often than not, the sex these women are having revolves around the pleasure of their male partner(s) and can feel like a chore or obligation. It is no wonder they lack interest in engaging in this kind of sexual experience. Educating these clients about the difference between spontaneous and responsive desire is a key part of my work. Individuals who experience spontaneous desire feel desire before sexual intimacy is initiated. Spontaneous desire emerges in anticipation of pleasure (Nagoski, 2024). I give my clients the example of someone walking down the street who suddenly feels sexual desire. Responsive desire is when an individual experiences desire after sexual intimacy has started or after being in a positive sexual context. Emily Nagoski, (2024) defines responsive desire as "the openness to exploring pleasure and seeing where it goes" (p. 23). The example I give my clients is to imagine being on a first date with someone while out to dinner. The conversation is invigorating, you feel good about yourself, and your date leans over and tickles your arm playfully. You feel a sense of desire or arousal. Then fast-forward a few years and imagine you are in a long-term relationship with this same person. It is 2:00 a.m. and you are changing your child's diaper, and your partner comes in and playfully tickles your arm. I imagine your response would be completely different. This is because one was a positive sexual context while the other was a negative sexual context. Same person and same touch, different context. A significant number of women experience responsive desire. As practitioners, it is important that we normalize responsive desire as well as spontaneous desire. One is not better than the other. Despite what our culture says, research shows that responsive desire, not spontaneous desire, is associated with long-term sexual satisfaction (Nagoski, 2024; Kleinplatz & Menard, 2020) Women who grew up in evangelical purity culture not only have to navigate the way they experience desire, but also an additional layer of unrealistic expectations, shame, fear, lack of experience, and embarrassment, just to name a few. I've found that the expectation of feeling spontaneous desire (combined with the messaging from purity culture) can significantly increase the lack of sexual desire and/or avoidance of sex. When sex is about giving pleasure to your husband and the belief that your wants, needs, desires, and pleasure are not important, it can feel like your humanity is erased. Women feeling obligated to have sex is very common in evangelical circles. Some of the reasons these women feel obligated to have sex are to keep their husbands from sinning sexually, feeling guilty for saying no, and trying to avoid their husbands becoming irritable and/or treating them poorly (Gregoire et al., 2021). Women who feel obligated to have sex with their husbands are 37 percent more likely to experience sexual pain and for 6.8 percent of these women, the pain is so intense that penetration is impossible (Gregoire et al., 2021).

I would like to focus on three vaginal pain disorders that I've found are prevalent in women exposed to purity culture: dyspareunia, vulvodynia, and vaginismus. One study conducted with evangelical women found that 32.3 percent experienced some form of sexual pain, 22.6 percent of which was related to vaginismus or dyspareunia (Gregoire et al., 2021). While there are other types of vaginal pain disorders that women from this population experience, these are the three that I have encountered most frequently in my work as a certified sex therapist. When an individual experiences pain before, during, or after sex, it is called dyspareunia. Fifteen percent of women in America experience genital pain that has no definite etiology or treatment, known as vulvodynia (Simonelli et al., 2014; Graziottin & Murina, 2011b). Women with vulvodynia have described their pain as a burning sensation or the feeling of being cut with a knife. Vulvodynia can cause dyspareunia and vice versa, which can create a cyclical relationship that can reduce the size of the vaginal entrance, which can cause inflammation and/or damage (Graziottin & Murina, 2011a). Dyspareunia is genital pain experienced before, during, or after vaginal penetration.

Studies have found that between 12 percent and 17 percent of women who seek out sex therapy have vaginismus (Hirst et al., 1996; Spector & Carey, 1990). Vaginismus is a sexual disorder in which the pubococcygeus (PC) muscle spasms involuntarily, making vaginal penetration painful and at times impossible (American Psychiatric Association, 2000). Women with vaginismus can experience pain upon genital touching around the vaginal opening, the vulvar vestibulum, and/or the perineum (American Psychiatric Association, 2000; Graziottin, 2006). This pain can last a couple of minutes or for some women, days (American Psychiatric Association, 2000). Many women who experience pain due to vaginismus and dyspareunia can develop a fear of sex or vaginal penetration because of the pain they experience (American Psychiatric Association, 2013). The exact causes of vaginismus are not yet known, but a number of studies have found that being raised in a religious environment where sex is viewed as vulgar, immoral, and shameful increases the likelihood of a woman experiencing vaginismus (Lewis et al., 2004). Women who have a fear of losing their bodily integrity and are taught to remain virgins until marriage may exhibit higher rates of vaginismus (Cotter, 2015). Women with vaginismus fear that vaginal penetration through sexual intercourse will cause pain (Reissing et al., 2003). "Women with vaginismus experience lower levels of sexual desire, arousal, and pleasure, and experience fewer orgasms during sexual intercourse" (Mizrahi, 2018, p. 18).

Any therapy that is supportive and encouraging can be an effective form of treatment for women who have vaginismus (Reissing et al, 2003). Sex therapy can be very effective with women who experience pain before, during, or after sex. During treatment, a sex therapist should help the client redefine their sexual experiences, help the client implement sexual boundaries, and encourage the client to take control of their sexual experiences, moving forward at their own pace. Eighty percent of participants in a study conducted by Hawton and Catalan (2007) had a positive outcome after attending sex therapy for vaginismus. Sex therapists provide psychosexual education about sexual anatomy and human sexuality. Religious women who have vaginismus often lack knowledge about sexuality due to a lack of education and sexual freedom (ter Kuile et al., 2009). Because these women often grew up in a sex-negative society, they have very little knowledge about their bodies, pleasure, or sex. Sex-negative societies value sex for procreation and not pleasure. Most people who come from a sex-negative culture are discouraged from seeking help for any sexual difficulties or dysfunctions out of fear that professionals may mistreat their condition (Mizrahi, 2018; Bhavsar & Bhugra, 2013). If rates of sexual pain are higher in women when they lack education or believe unhealthy narratives, then part of their healing journey must be challenging what they were taught and the beliefs they have. Challenging these messages and/or beliefs does not require the individual to change them, but instead gives them permission to choose which messages and beliefs they want to keep or disconnect from.

The medical field typically treats vaginismus with vaginal dilation, which helps women gain control of their pelvic floor to reduce their involuntary muscle spasms (Cotter, 2015). Dilators come in a variety of sizes and are made of medical-grade plastic. Women are instructed to start with a smaller-sized dilator that they manually insert into the vagina to expand the vagina. During dilation, the woman follows a program given to her by her doctor in which she trains her PC muscles by squeezing and relaxing them. These exercises help her train her PC muscles so she can override and relax any involuntary muscle contractions (Binik, 2009). The woman slowly works her way up through different sizes of dilators until she is able to insert a dilator that is similar to the size of a penis (if her goal is penile penetration). Because so many women with vaginismus fear having anything in their vagina because it may cause pain, dilators help desensitize their vagina and overcome the psychological blocks that were keeping them from being able to insert anything into their vaginas. Many evangelical women feel uncomfortable with this form of treatment because they were taught that putting anything in their vaginas other than their husband's penis was unacceptable and even sinful. They were discouraged from exploring their own bodies, let alone inserting anything into their bodies. I tell my clients who have vulvodynia or vaginismus that their vulva and vagina are doing what they can to protect them. Ward and Ogden (1994) conducted a study on 89 women where it was determined that vaginismus should not be thought of as a psychosexual problem, but instead should be viewed as a psychosocial experience that allowed the woman to protect herself. They argued that the vaginal spasms were the way that the body protected the woman and prevented vaginal penetration.

When an individual is raised to protect their purity and virginity, and to avoid pleasure or sexuality outside of marriage, it is easy to develop anxiety. The body holds this anxiety and one way that the body can protect itself is by making sex painful so that it won't happen. This is a trauma and/or fear response. When working with clients who have vaginismus or vulvodynia, I start by helping them create a trusting relationship with their vulva. Each morning, I ask the client to hold or touch their vulva, allowing themselves to feel the warmth of their hand on the vulva. I ask them to say hello to their vulva and tell their vulva what they appreciate about the vulva and what they want the vulva to know and/or believe. This builds a relationship between the client and their vulva, helping decrease their fear, shame, or disgust. Once the client is able to create a trusting relationship with their vulva, I encourage them to look at the vulva in a mirror and to draw what they see. Many of these clients have never explored or looked at their vulva, so this can be embarrassing or difficult. We take things slow and go at their pace. Once the client can connect with and look at their vulva, the next step is exploration of the vulva to discover what gives them pleasure. This builds confidence in the client and in their ability to understand their vulva and what gives them pleasure.

Other symptoms that can go along with sexual dysfunction for women who grew up in purity culture are immense guilt and shame, fear around living outside of traditional gender roles, fear of going to hell for participating in sexual acts outside of marriage, self-disgust, and lack of trust in self and others (Anderson, 2021). There is a definite link between gender-role expectations and sexual dysfunction (Bhavsar & Bhugra, 2013). Some forms of sexual dysfunction last a lifetime, while others are situational or develop later in life. Studies have found that there is a correlation between being religious or being exposed to religious teachings and/or beliefs and increased levels of sexual dysfunction. Purity culture taught that healthy sex was for married heterosexuals, for procreation, that it re-volved around male pleasure, and that it was the responsibility of women to satisfy the sexual needs of their male partners. These messages created expectations and pressure for women that often turned into performance anxiety. When someone is in a state of performance anxiety, they focus on specific acts or techniques, which makes it difficult to focus on plea-sure. The brain is the largest sex organ and when someone is in a state of performance anxiety, they are primarily in their head, which affects their ability to connect to their body or experience pleasure in their body. If your head is not in the game, you are less likely to experience pleasure or connection during sex.

When talking to my clients about fulfilling sex, I encourage them to focus on desire, pleasure, and satisfaction. I describe sex as an ice-cream cone with three scoops. The first scoop is desire—do I desire my partner in any way and/or do they desire me? Pleasure is the second scoop—did I experience any form of pleasure during the sexual experience? Satisfac-tion is the third scoop—after the sexual experience is over, was there any part of it that I would like to experience again? Nowhere in that ice-cream cone was an orgasm or what their body looked like or if they moved the right way. Most of the time when we have one, two, or three scoops of ice cream, a cherry will show up. The cherry is the orgasm that can top off the already amazing ice-cream cone. No one goes to an ice-cream shop and orders a cone with only a cherry in it. We need the ice cream because that's what makes the ice-cream cone have substance and taste good. When we look at sex like an ice-cream cone made up of three scoops and possibly a cherry, it takes the focus off performance and puts it on the entire experience. It also normalizes that sometimes you might only have one or two scoops of ice cream, which can still be a tasty treat.

Sexuality is very black and white in evangelical purity culture. There is a right and wrong way to approach every aspect of sexuality with very little room for flexibility. Evangelical culture teaches that sexual fulfill-ment is something men need, and women may enjoy, which would be a bonus. When this is the message that individuals hear, it is no surprise that women don't expect to enjoy sex and that their male partners don't think there's anything wrong if she doesn't like sex (Gregoire et al., 2021). Women are taught to control and often suppress their thoughts, desires, and feelings around sex with the goal of remaining pure. This kind of sexual framework can easily create sexual dysfunction in women because it disconnects them from pleasure and their bodies. The black-and-white thinking around sexuality also creates a lot of unrealistic expectations for women. They have the expectation that they should remain emotion-ally and physically pure until marriage and then magically turn into a sexual goddess who knows exactly what to do as a sexual partner. When unrealistic expectations are not met, resentments are often created. Imagine waiting to express your sexuality until your wedding night because you believed that it was the way you could show God and your partner that you loved them. Imagine being promised this wonderful experience filled with love, connection, passion, and ecstasy if you remained pure. And then imagine those promises not coming true and the amount of disappointment and confusion that could ensue. Instead of looking at the promises and unrealistic expectations they were given and how they were failed by the system, many of these women blamed themselves. How could they not when they were taught that everyone was born sinful? This is what happened to so many evangelical women who grew up in purity culture. Instead of challenging and questioning what they had been taught, they turned inward and blamed themselves, in turn creating shame. This shame can be held in the body and can show up in the form of sexual dysfunction. I want to share two case studies from my work as a sex therapist to demonstrate how to work with sexual dysfunction that was caused by the teachings or purity culture. The names, ages, and details about these clients have been changed to protect their identity.

CASE STUDY #1

Amy showed up to her first therapy session in jeans and a large sweatshirt. She did not have any makeup on and was slightly slumped over as if she was trying to make herself shorter and smaller than she actually was. Her voice was quiet, and I could tell she was nervous. As we started our first session, Amy told me that she had come to sex therapy because she had been married for four years and had not been able to have penetrative sex with her husband because of the pain she experienced when they tried any form of penetration in the vagina. Amy was raised in a conservative Christian home in the South where abstinence before marriage was expected. Amy was the oldest of five children and described herself as the peacemaker in her family. She spent much of her childhood helping her overly stressed mom raise her four younger siblings, and she had been homeschooled until high school. Amy didn't have many friends in high school and kept to herself. Most of her social interactions took place at church and in youth group. Amy got good grades in school and worked her way through college since her parents were unable to help her out financially. Amy had recently graduated with her nursing degree and had a job as a nurse at a local hospital. Amy stated that she had only had two boyfriends before she met her husband in college and that they had been relatively short relationships that both ended because of her unwillingness to have a sexual relationship outside of marriage. Amy met her husband, Jordan, in college and felt drawn to him right away. He had not grown up in a religious home and struggled with anxiety and depression. Amy felt that she could help him and found herself emotionally supporting him as she had supported her siblings. After dating for a few weeks, Amy told Jordan that she wanted to wait to have sex until they got married, and he was supportive. Jordan had not had penetrative sex before they got married, although he had a lot more experience with sexual play than Amy did. They dated for six months before getting married at Amy's church. She told me how excited she was to wear her white dress on her wedding day because she knew she had followed God's commands. She was anxious about having sex with Jordan but believed that everything would work out and that it would be a positive experience. On their honeymoon they tried to have sex, but Amy was extremely anxious and felt overwhelmed. When Jordan tried to penetrate her Amy experienced a shooting pain in her vulva and vagina that caused her to cry. No matter how slowly or gently they went, Jordan was unable to insert his finger or his penis into Amy. Amy and Jordan decided to focus on other forms of physical touch and intimacy for the rest of the honeymoon with the hopes that sex would naturally happen in time. This continued for the next four years and each time they would try to have sex, Amy experienced pain, which then turned into embarrassment and then shame. Amy desperately wanted to have children. She felt that she was failing at her wifely duties and that her body was broken. She told me that she didn't understand why she wasn't able to have sex when she had followed God's word and had remained pure. As we continued to work together in therapy, I diagnosed Amy with vaginismus and anxiety. Vaginismus happens when the muscles in the vagina and pelvic floor involuntarily contract, making it almost impossible to penetrate. Vaginismus often has a psychological cause, such as anxiety, trauma, and/or shame. Amy felt broken and found herself speaking about and to herself in a demeaning and shameful way. Having an official diagnosis of vaginismus and knowing that she was not alone in her difficulties gave Amy hope for the first time in years. I explained that vaginismus was the way that her body/vagina was protecting her from what they felt was unsafe and/or bad. I had her write a letter to her vulva telling the vulva what she felt and what she needed. This allowed her to connect to her vulva and process her anger and sadness. Instead of being angry at her vulva, we reframed it in a way that Amy was able to thank her vulva for doing what it thought it needed to do. The messages around modesty, sin, purity, and abstinence were deeply ingrained in Amy. She had spent much of her life avoiding any sexual thoughts or feelings to follow the rules. While she logically knew that she was allowed to have sex with her husband, emotionally she was reacting from a place of avoidance, fear, and shame. I helped her see that there wasn't a magical switch that she could flip to go from anti-sex to sex positive. We identified the messages that she had received about her body, gender, and sexuality growing up. I had Amy think about these messages and write them down. Next to each message I had her write down where that message had come from—if it was a specific person, place, experience, movie, etc. I then had her read each message out loud and notice what her body felt like when she heard the message. Where did she feel the response in her body? Was there a sound, memory, smell, or color associated with that message? I then asked Amy if that was a message that was adding to the quality of her life or if it was holding her back in some way. I told her that a belief is typically something that we have heard repeatedly over time until it becomes something we embrace as fact. Beliefs are fluid and can be changed. We do not have to be held captive by beliefs and are in control of the beliefs we choose each and every day. I had Amy write down the beliefs and messages that she wanted to release on tiny pieces of paper. We then read each one out loud and threw it into a firepit. After burning the old belief and/or message I had Amy write down the belief that she wanted to incorporate into her life on a vision board that she hung in her bedroom. Each day she would read these new beliefs out loud while getting dressed for work. I encouraged Amy to work with a pelvic floor physical therapist who taught her how to relax the muscles in her pelvic floor through the use of biofeedback and dilators. The pelvic floor physical therapist taught Amy about her pelvic floor and how it worked. I used psychosexual education to introduce Amy to her sexual anatomy through the use of diagrams, books, and a vulva puppet that she could hold and touch. I explained how arousal worked in the mind and the body, discussing the difference between spontaneous desire and responsive desire. I encouraged Amy to incorporate nonsexual but pleasurable touch into her daily life. As Amy explored her senses and her body, she kept a journal of everything that gave her pleasure. We focused on the different types of pleasure, emotional, intellectual, physical, sexual, and relational. I introduced Amy to mindfulness through the use of guided imagery and deep-breathing techniques. As Amy gave herself permission to explore her body and found what gave her pleasure, I encouraged her to share what she was discovering with Jordan. Amy's confidence began to improve, and she carried herself differently. Instead of hiding herself and wearing clothes that covered every inch of her, she wore clothes that made her feel beautiful. She held her head up and smiled more. Once Amy got to a place where she felt like she understood herself and her sexuality, we invited Jordan to join us in therapy. We used sensate focus activities that took away the pressure to have sex. Using Barry McCarthy's (2015) five gears of touch, the couple figured out what kinds of touch they each enjoyed while focusing on one gear at a time. They focused on playfulness, affection, and pleasure, which allowed them to create a sense of physical and emotional safety. Over the next year, I worked alongside Amy and Jordan until they were finally able to have pain-free, penetrative sex. They were both able to increase their confidence and ultimately create a couple's sexual style that revolved around pleasure, play, and communication. They are now the proud parents of three beautiful children.

CASE STUDY #2

Tara had an outgoing, bubbly personality with an infectious laugh. I could tell she loved to be the center of attention and that she was probably the life of any party she went to. In our first session together, she told me that she had been raised by strict, evangelical parents and that her dad was a pastor. Tara couldn't remember a time when she wasn't at church as a child. As a pastor's kid there was a lot of pressure to be perfect because her behavior was a direct representation of her father and his ministry. When Tara was six, one of the church deacons began to spend a lot of time with her. He would take her out to breakfast after church on Sundays while her dad preached at the second service. The deacon gave Tara a lot of attention and told her that he loved and cherished her. Eventually the deacon began touching Tara inappropriately on their car rides to and from breakfast. He threatened to tell everyone at the church how bad she was if she told anyone. This abuse continued for three years until the deacon moved away. Sex was not really discussed in Tara's home or at church, so she kept the secret and pretended that everything was OK. She knew that sex was only for married people and that she was not supposed to have sex before marriage. Sexual attention was not in alignment with God and modesty was of the utmost importance. When Tara hit puberty, her body flooded with all kinds of new feelings and sensations. She longed to be seen, heard, touched, and loved. While she knew her parents loved her, they did not show love through physical affection. Tara found herself looking for that love in relationships with boys at school. By ninth grade Tara had developed quite a reputation at school. While at church and around her family, she followed the rules and kept up the perfect Christian image, but she was very different at school. Tara craved attention and soon figured out that the easiest way to get attention was to have sex with boys. In the beginning of these relationships, she felt confident and craved attention, but once she had sex with a boy she found herself shutting down and leaving her body. Whenever she was done having sex with someone, Tara would think about how her behavior was a sin and that she would definitely go to hell for it. Tara would ruminate on this thought for days until she could find someone new to get attention from, which would give her a break for a short time until the cycle started all over again. Tara focused on giving pleasure in order to receive attention. It became a transaction. Sex was not pleasurable, but instead the only way that she knew how to get the attention she had longed for her entire life. Tara got pregnant when she was 17, which came as a shock to her parents. They were so wrapped up in their lives at the church that they had no idea Tara had been having sex. Tara's father was livid when he found out she was pregnant and insisted that she and the father of the child get married. Tara and Ryan got married and had their son, Ian. Tara told me that she needed help because whenever she thought about sex or even tried to have sex, her body would shut down. She felt that Ryan was having sex to her body, but not with Tara. Tara was unable to stay present during sex or experience pleasure. Ryan complained about her lack of interest in sex and had threatened to leave her because his needs were not being met. She was also struggling with guilt about not being a good mom because she had been so young when she got pregnant. She didn't know who she was or what she wanted, let alone how to raise a child. Tara was also angry because she felt that her parents had always chosen the church and God over her. They had failed to protect her from the deacon or even notice what was happening in her life. She ultimately felt that she was not lovable. I validated Tara's feelings about sex and let her know that that her lack of sexual desire was not because something was wrong with her, but instead was from the trauma she had been carrying around with her since childhood. I had her read several books on sexual trauma that helped normalize her feelings and reassured her that she was not alone in her experiences. I had her write a letter to the deacon from her church, telling him everything she had always wanted to say to him. She then read it out loud and burned the letter in her firepit at home. This was her way of giving her inner child the closure she so desperately needed. I asked Tara to write a letter to her inner child, letting her know that what happened was not her fault and that she deserved to have caregivers who protected her. Whenever Tara felt triggered, I had her identify what the core feeling was, how old the feeling was, and what it needed to hear. I had her speak to each part that came forward as the grown-up that she had needed when she was a child, which helped build trust between her inner child and her adult self. I had Tara write down what she had hoped her parents would be like and what she had needed them to be. I then had her write down who they actually were as parents. Tara then looked at the disparity between the parents she had wanted and needed and the parents they were, giving herself permission to grieve the fact that the parents she always wanted did not exist. A big part of this healing involved Tara letting herself accept that her parents were not what she needed because they were flawed and human, not because she was not lovable or good enough. As we worked through the painful relationship she had with her parents, she implemented some healthy boundaries with her family. I encouraged her to focus on finding people she could rely on and trust, who could become her chosen family. We looked at her sexual development and how sexuality had been introduced to her much earlier than it should've been in ways that were abusive and non-consensual. I taught her about healthy sexual development and what that should've looked like for her. We then took sex off the table while she focused on self-exploration and curiosity so she could figure out what she liked instead of doing what her partner wanted. I encouraged her to slow down and focus on sensations when touching herself or being touched by others. We looked at what motivated Tara to want sex/intimacy, what she wanted to feel during sex, and what good sex would look like, feel like, sound like, taste like, and smell like. The focus became less about her partner and what he wanted and more about what Tara was feeling and what gave her pleasure. This allowed her to rewrite her sexual script and embrace the kind of touch and sexuality that she wanted moving forward. Through our work together, Tara decided to embrace spirituality instead of organized religion and was able to slow down, embrace pleasure, and learn how to be present during sex.

In both case studies there were multiple layers that we had to work through together. Each client is different and has their own story. Gathering the information and coming up with a plan of action with the client is essential in building rapport and trust with the client. Some of the tools or techniques that work with one client may not work with another, which is why approaching this work from a psychosocial perspective is so important. I tell my clients that I cannot fix their problem or situation. My job is to give them every tool that I have in my toolbox so that they leave therapy with tools that work for them. It is up to the client to use the tools they are given. I always reiterate that you get out of therapy what you put into therapy.

7

✝

LGBTQIA+ and Purity Culture

While I do not have the space in this book to address the impact of purity culture on individuals from the LGBTQIA+ community in full, I believe it is important to briefly address and discuss how this community was impacted by the messaging of purity culture and the teachings of the evangelical Christian church. In all the research that I conducted for this book, I found very little information about the effects of purity culture on members of the LGBTQIA+ community. There were a few books written by members of the community who came out in adulthood, but there is a significant need for more information and research on this topic. As someone who identifies as pansexual and who is in a same-sex relationship, I can speak from my personal experience, but this in no way embodies the experiences of everyone in this population. There is a great need for research in this area so that we can better help people who not only survived the teachings of purity culture, but also came out as not heterosexual and/or monogamous. The teachings of evangelical Christian purity culture were adamant that heterosexual, monogamous relationships were what God intended for his people and that anything outside of that relationship model was sinful. They believed that God made Adam and Eve, not Adam and Steve, which in turn meant that only heterosexual relationships were in alignment with God's plan. While there are many churches that disagree with this way of thinking and that have embraced members from the LGBTQIA+ community, there are still many Christians and Christian denominations who do not. Purity culture taught that being gay was a lifestyle choice and that people are not born gay. Making a distinction between sex and sexuality was a way that the evangelical church reinforced the belief that sexuality in and of itself was not sinful, while the act of sex or sexual thoughts were (Roberts, 2020). This framework helped shape purity culture and was used to weaponize the LGBTQIA+ community. In essence, choosing the LGBTQIA+ "lifestyle" was not itself sinful, but acting on it was. Evangelical theologian Stanley Grenz encouraged people to treat same-sex feelings, attractions, urges, desires, and longings as temptations to be mastered, instead of sins to be confessed (Gardner, 2011). The evangelical church encouraged people from the LGBTQIA+ community to remain celibate because their desires were outside of God's perfect design for love, marriage, and sex. I remember hearing the statement, "love the sinner, not the sin" when the topic of same-sex relationships came up. Erika Allison, a queer reverend who grew up in evangelical purity culture, states in her book *Gay the Pray Away* that "religion is one of the biggest culprits of implanting, harmful messaging into the hearts, minds, and psyches of the queer community" (Erika Allison, 2021, p. 2). When the church told individuals that who they were, what they desired, and who they were attracted to was somehow wrong or bad, it created fear and shame. Allison (2021) states that the rejection, judgment, or use of manipulation to change who someone is at their core is called identity harm. Identity harm can make someone believe that they are not deserving of love or are not enough just as they are. Instead, who they are is broken, wrong, bad, or out of alignment with God. Many LGBTQIA+ individuals flew under the radar while growing up in purity culture. They didn't have to worry about having sex outside of marriage because they may not have been attracted to the opposite sex or may have had no interest in sex at all because they were asexual. Pledging to remain abstinent until marriage didn't make a lot of sense to individuals who were gay because at that time gay marriage was not legalized in most states. Abstinence groups like Silver Ring Thing and True Love Waits rarely addressed or focused on purity among LGBTQIA+ youth due to the overall belief that same-sex relationships were sinful (Gardner, 2011). These groups did encourage LGBTQIA+ youth to commit to abstinence, but since they believed this was such a small percentage of the population, they did not feel they needed to spend a lot of time discussing it (Gardner, 2011). Since a core message was to remain pure and not be sexual with the opposite sex, it was easy to hide one's true sexual orientation if it fell outside of heterosexuality.

Close friendships between members of the same sex were encouraged in purity culture because having a support system and people to hold you accountable was important. I remember falling asleep next to my best friend in high school while she would caress my hand and snuggle me. No one in my community was worried about two girls having a sleepover; they never imagined that I had romantic feelings for her. I was simply expressing love to a good friend. In those moments when we would be falling asleep, I would convince myself that this was normal for best friends to do and that the feelings I had for her would eventually go away.

Exodus International was the largest ex-gay organization at the height of purity culture; they encouraged the use of conversion therapy or reparative therapy as a way to deal with the LGBTQIA+ community. The focus of conversion therapy was to shift the sexual orientation of an individual toward heterosexuality. Conversion therapy taught participants that gender and sexual orientation were malleable because in their opinion gender and sexuality were socially formed (Gerber, 2008). The goal of conversion therapy was to help free people from their ungodly desires and sins so they could become the person who God wanted them to be. Being same-sex-attracted was viewed as a moral and psychological issue as well as being sinful. Ex-gay organizations believed that same-sex attraction resulted from a lack of clear gender identity often caused by a disruption in the relationship with their caregiver of the same sex. These individuals then grew up feeling unsatisfied with their same-sex connections, which during puberty became eroticized (Gerber, 2008). One of the ways to "fix" this problem was to create healthy, nonsexual connections with people of the same sex so they could heal the disconnection they experienced in childhood and become heterosexual just as God intended. In essence, forming close same-sex friendships along with gender training would heal the individual so they could embrace heterosexuality (Gerber, 2008). According to the Williams Institute at UCLA, more than 700,000 adults (half of whom were under the age of 18) were exposed to conversion therapy (Erika Allison, 2021). The tools and modalities used in conversion therapy not only were harmful to participants but have all been rejected by the American Psychiatric Association and other reputable organizations within the mental health field (Erika Allison, 2021). In many states it is illegal to provide or offer conversion therapy, although it still goes on in churches and in the offices of Christian counselors all over the country. I believe we have only just started to scratch the surface of how conversion therapy and the messages of purity culture affected members of the LGBTQIA+ community. This population deserves to be acknowledged and heard to break these cycles of abuse.

Part II

MOVING INTO
THE CURRICULUM

Whether you plan to use the information in this book and curriculum one-on-one with a client or in a group setting, it is important to note that you as the practitioner are welcome to use the information and activities in whatever way you feel would be most impactful. Some clients may not need to learn about or discuss every topic covered in the curriculum. If you plan to use this curriculum in a group setting, I encourage you to interview participants prior to starting the group to make sure that they are in a relatively similar part of their healing journey. You would not want to mix clients who are just starting out on their journey with individuals who are a few years into healing. I trust that as the practitioner you will navigate this on a client-by-client basis.

8

✛

Class 1

Origins of Purity Culture

OBJECTIVES

- Participants will identify the need and purpose of the curriculum.
- Participants will examine and discuss the rules/norms of the class series.
- Participants will create their "garden schemas" and identify preexisting schema elements.

GREETING AND WELCOME

Welcome to the seven-part class series regarding the effects of purity culture on sexuality. You will learn strategies to deconstruct its messaging to better understand and embrace sexual pleasure. This curriculum is primarily intended for women who experienced the negative messaging and effects of purity culture. This curriculum is also a resource for the mental health professionals who want to be better equipped to work with clients who experienced life in the evangelical Christian purity movement.

Most secular mental health professionals are not specifically trained to work with religious clients despite the large number of psychotherapy clients who have experienced harmful religious indoctrination. It is important to start out by saying that this curriculum is not anti-God, anti-church, or anti-spirituality, but is anti-dogma. Dogmatic religion is one that does not honor the thoughts or feelings of people. It is one that is static, without room for growth or development (Winell, 1993). The nature of dogmatic religion is to separate from everything else because it claims to have the only truth. Therefore, no matter how altruistic it claims to be, a rigid religion will produce judgment, since there will always be others who believe differently. Judgment will inevitably lead to discrimination and persecution. Dogma does not allow us to come together to understand our shared humanity (Winell, 1993). A dogmatic framework operates on a dualistic basis of right and wrong, reward and punishment.

This curriculum is not intended to change the religious beliefs of the participants, but rather it seeks to create a safe space where they are able to decrease religious sexual shame and navigate how to combine their faith (if the participant maintains a faith) and their sexuality after being given accurate information about female sexual anatomy, sex, pleasure, and sexuality. All participants are required to attend individual or couples therapy with a licensed mental health professional in conjunction with attending this psychoeducational group in order to process any emotional conflicts or difficulties that could arise. Deconstruction or challenging one's core beliefs can impact an individual's entire family system, which is why outside professional support is required. Due to the sensitive topics of this curriculum and the time constraints of the individual classes, there will not be sufficient time or resources in this psychoeducational group to process all of the thoughts and emotions that may arise. All participants are encouraged to take notes or write down thoughts that come up during the group to process those thoughts outside of the group with their therapist and/or support system.

No matter where you are in your healing I am excited to work with you on this journey of reclaiming your sexual identity.

GROUND RULES

As we begin this journey together, it is important that we identify some ground rules for our group that will encourage safety and unity during our time together. Some of the ground rules that are required are privacy and protection of information shared in the group; respect for all members' ideas, experiences, questions, and lifestyles; and space for all voices to be heard. Does anyone else have any ideas they would like to add to the ground rules? (Have everyone add to the list on a giant paper on the wall. Once that is complete and everyone is in agreement with the rules, have all members sign the paper.)

For our first activity, I would like each of you to take a piece of paper and a pen and write down the answers to these three questions: (1) What is your name and what motivated you to attend this class? (2) What are two or three words or images that describe your experience with purity culture? and (3) What do you hope to get out of this experience?

Consent is one of the cornerstones of this group. At its most basic level, consent is the giving of permission for something to occur. According to Hardy and Easton (2017), "Consent is the active collaboration for the benefit, well-being, and pleasure of all persons" (p. 23). With that in mind, if anyone would be interested in sharing their answers, please feel free to do so now. Conversely, if you would prefer not to share your responses, that choice will always be respected. Everyone learns and processes in different ways. I assure you that you will be given the freedom to choose how you participate during this class. We will be spending a significant amount of time together over the next few weeks. It is my hope that you are all able to learn something about yourselves and one another during this process.

Today's session will specifically focus on the history and core beliefs of evangelical Christian purity culture to help us better understand when, why, and how it came to be. This curriculum was designed for women who grew up in and/or were exposed to purity teachings, messages, and programs created by the evangelical Christian church starting in the 1980s through the early 2000s. This curriculum has also been created to help educate therapists and mental health professionals who wish to understand what purity culture is and how to best serve clients who lived through it.

Because of the intense (and often incorrect/inaccurate) delivery of purity culture messages, specifically to youth, many individuals exposed to purity messages now report difficulties with shame, religious sexual shame, lack of sexual desire, sexual dysfunction, and/or difficulty with constructing a positive body image. Purity culture was only able to thrive in ignorance because it was based on false theological, emotional, spiritual, and physical claims (Emily J. Allison, 2021).

During these seven sessions, participants will be given the opportunity to identify the messages they received about sexual behaviors, sexual morality, their bodies, pleasure, and their roles as women. Once these messages and beliefs have been identified, participants will be given the opportunity to decide which of these they would like to preserve and which of them they would like to discard. This process is called deconstruction, which according to Josh de Keijzer (2019), is the opposite of construction and destruction; it is being able to identify the constructed elements of your faith before taking them apart to see how they were constructed.

Deconstruction is more than questioning one's religious beliefs; it is realizing that all reality is constructed. It is the process of realizing and accepting that all doctrines, rules, values, and morals that we are taught as truths are, in fact, things simply constructed and created by humans. Think back to when you were growing up in purity culture and ask yourself how you knew what you knew about God. What happens inside of you when you're invited to separate God, the true, mysterious, unknowable God, from everything that you were told about God? Does this feel liberating? Does this feel scary, like everything you've known is being pulled out from under your feet? Or does this feel like something you've always intuitively known? (Take time between each question to let participants process and respond.)

While this can initially feel freeing because you can separate God from what you were told to believe about God, you may also need to mourn and grieve the loss of what you believed, how you thought the world worked, and ultimately what you learned about God (de Keijzer, 2019). Inerrancy is the belief that the Bible is without error and that it had to be without error in order to be true (Barr, 2021). Barr (2021) argues, "Inerrancy creates an atmosphere of fear. Any question raised about biblical accuracy must be completely answered or completely rejected to prevent the fragile fabric of faith from unraveling" (p. 190). Many individuals who grew up in evangelical Christianity are scared to question the doctrines of sexuality taught to them by the church because they feel that by questioning the orthodoxy, they are questioning God (Emily J. Allison, 2021).

Emily Nagoski, author of *Come as You Are* (2015a), compares this awakening, evaluating, and mourning process to tending a garden. We are each born with a plot of fertile land and your brain and your body are the soil. When you are a child, your parents and your culture plant the seeds of language, attitudes, knowledge, and habits about love, safety, your body, and sex. As you continue to grow and develop, you take on more responsibility for your garden. You may notice that some of the seeds that your family and culture planted are beautiful and nourishing while others are toxic, unhealthy, or dangerous. Even if your family planted beneficial seeds, you have to deal with weeds from our sex-negative culture that represent shame and sexual stigmas.

Now that you are an adult, you get to choose what you want to keep in your garden. You may have to go row by row to look at each seed, plant, or weed that is in your garden. As you do this, you will decide what needs to be dug out and what you want to keep. You may ask, "Why do I have to do this when I didn't plant any of it?"

I agree it is not fair that you have to do this hard and often painful work. The people in your life who planted these seeds didn't ask for your consent to plant them in your garden. In truth, many of them probably just planted the same seeds in your garden that they had planted in their own gardens. They probably didn't know they could plant something different (Nagoski, 2015b).

Not every plant in the garden is bad, but we will definitely need to do some weeding during the time we have together. We will focus on how to identify the difference between weeds and healthy plants, while also learning some strategies for cutting them back and in some instances pulling them out. In addition, we'll work to add new plants to your garden that will sustain you for the rest of your life—plants that bring joy, nourishment, and pleasure.

BACKGROUND

Today we will start with some background on evangelical Christianity and how pervasive the messaging of purity culture was. This information will demonstrate how individuals were immersed in the messaging from the church, the government, the school, marketing, and their families.

While perceptions of the modern American evangelical Christian are abundant in society (frequently stemming from their political activism), one may be surprised to learn that American evangelical Christianity has its roots in early British Protestant reforms dating back to the eighteenth century. Known as the First Great Awakening, Protestant sects (the main branches of the Reformation) began espousing similar views on humanity's eternal battle with sin and temptation. Rather than scold parishioners post-sin, these sects, which later collectively became known as evangelicals, sought to preemptively encourage and assist their members in abstaining from sin and temptation (Hart, 2002). In addition to this preemptive approach, this movement was marked by a fervent need for individuals to be "born again." Hart (2002) notes that revival events of this period focused on preaching in a way "designed to bring hearers to a point of crisis, at which they despaired over their sinfulness and experienced the love of God in an immediate way" (p. 7).

Once a community professed to be "born again," leading revivalists focused heavily on encouraging "holy living." This "holy living" was marked by "behaving in a visibly devout manner, whether by abstaining from certain worldly activities or by performing righteous deeds" (Hart, 2002, p. 7). While each denomination went through a variety of reforms over the following two centuries, it is important to note that they remained separate entities rather than coalescing as one evangelical church.

The American evangelical church is now described as a movement focused on "witnessing the gospel" (Sweeney, 2005, p. 24). Douglas Sweeney describes American evangelicals as a combination of Christian believers who also happen to be members of various Protestant denominations including, but not limited to, Anglicans, Methodists, Pentecostals, Lutherans, and Anabaptist evangelicals. Sweeney (2005) admits, "We have no card-carrying membership, not even an official membership list" (p. 13).

In Alister McGrath's book, *Evangelicalism and the Future of Christianity* (1996), McGrath describes evangelicals as subscribing to six core convictions. These convictions can be summarized as a belief in God, a belief in Jesus Christ as the savior of humanity, a belief in the existence of the Holy Spirit, the need for a personal conversion experience, the need for evangelism (preaching the gospel) to the world, and a belief in the importance of the Christian community for fellowship and spiritual growth (McGrath, 1996). According to the National Association of Evangelicals, one must uphold the Bible as their ultimate authority, must confess the centrality of Christ's atonement, must believe in being born again, and must spread the good news of the gospel in order to be an evangelical (Kobes Du Mez, 2020). It is these core convictions that helped the various denominations unite a movement around topics such as purity in order to thwart society's perceived ills. According to Anderson (2015), "Sexual purity has become the one means by which the evangelical church separates itself from the world" (p. 20).

Joe Carter (2019) of the Gospel Coalition describes the purity culture movement as a product of attempts in the 1980s and 1990s to address pressing sexual topics like the AIDS epidemic, all-time-high teen pregnancy rates, and a dramatic increase in premarital sex rates.

While evangelical churches have preached the need for holy living for centuries, one cannot deny the societal impact of the shift in the American evangelical church that occurred in the mid-1970s. It wasn't until then that the American evangelical church shifted from focusing on influencing internal congregations to influencing national politics, culminating in the passage of the Adolescent Family Life Act (AFLA) signed into law by President Ronald Reagan in 1981 (Colvin, 2020). The AFLA was the product of Senator Jeremiah Denton and Senator Orrin Hatch. Seeking to specifically address teen pregnancy, Denton and Hatch sought to mandate that the federal government would promote "chastity and self-discipline" programs for teenagers (AFLA, as cited in Saul, 1998, para. 7). The AFLA's initial grants were used by religious groups to create curricula such as Sex Respect and the Silver Ring Thing. Initially intended to be a program that provided teens with information about sex, the *Sex Respect Student Workbook* (2019) came to be seen quite differently. Indeed, it was fraught with racial and homophobic bias, gender stereotyping, and fear tactics trying to convince teens just to say "no" to sex (Rethinking Schools, 2020).

In 1992, Richard Ross, a youth ministry consultant, was credited with creating the True Love Waits campaign for Lifeway, a Christian publisher (Lifeway, n.d.). Within a year, the Southern Baptist Convention had obtained 100,000 signed youth commitment cards from individuals pledging to abstain from premarital sex. Over the course of the next few years, rallies, media events, and conventions took place in the United States promoting the campaign. Churches and publishers began to notice the success of the True Love Waits campaign and began to create curricula, media, family events, and memorabilia to support the movement. With state school systems investing in and promoting abstinence-only sex education programs (using abundant federal funds thanks to the AFLA), American evangelical churches sought to reinforce the lessons taught while promoting additional non-secular themes to their congregants. These themes included an additional focus on the importance of remaining a virgin until marriage, avoiding sexual temptations, and for women, protecting men from sexual sin. These themes were reinforced through curriculum materials, pledges, events such as purity balls, and even purity rings designed to remind the wearer to remain pure (Rosenbloom, 2005).

According to Kobes Du Mez (2020), "Purity culture drew on teachings long championed by conservative evangelicals accustomed to upholding stringent standards of female sexual 'purity' while assigning men the responsibility of 'protecting' women and their chastity. Female modesty was a key component of purity culture. If men were created with nearly irrepressible God-given sex drives, it was up to women to rein in men's libidos" (p. 170). Josh Harris wrote the book *I Kissed Dating Goodbye* (1997), which was influenced by the writings of Elizabeth Elliot. In his book, Harris introduced a generation of adolescent Christians to what he called "biblical courtship," which was the idea that fathers were responsible for ensuring their daughters' purity until their wedding days (as cited in Kobes Du Mez, 2020, p. 171). On her wedding day, a woman would be handed over to her husband, who would then take on the burden of protecting her, providing for her, and supervising her (Kobes Du Mez, 2020). Kobes Du Mez (2020) notes, "A message of delayed gratification was at the heart of purity teachings for adolescent boys. Since wives served to gratify male desire, men only needed to wait until marriage to be rewarded with 'mindblowing' sex" (p. 170). *I Kissed Dating Goodbye* (1997) became the bible of the purity movement and sold more than one million copies (Kobes Du Mez, 2020).

In 1998, the first purity ball was hosted in Colorado Springs, Colorado, home of Focus on the Family Ministry. A purity ball is a formal dance attended by fathers and their adolescent daughters. According to Dianna Anderson (2015), the purpose of the purity ball was to emphasize the father's role in protecting the virginity of his daughter. Purity balls offered families the opportunity to enact their commitment to sexual purity through a public ceremony. Kobes Du Mez (2020) reports, "At these events, fathers provided a model of masculine headship by 'dating' their daughters, and girls pledged their sexual purity before their families and communities" (p. 171).

By 2003, abstinence-only education was the norm for the majority of public schools. While there was language in various federal funding bills prohibiting direct support of religious or faith-based lessons, the hunger for abstinence-only curricula led to a lack of oversight coupled with a willingness by Christian publishers to take whatever funding came their way (Anderson, 2015). These initial abstinence-only and purity programs were heralded as successes, and in fact, a 2009 CDC study noted a significant decline in sexual activity for girls ages 15 to 17 and boys ages 15 to 18 (Carter, 2019). Additional evidence from a study completed in 2009 found that the actual sexual behaviors of teens who took purity pledges did not differ dramatically from the sexual behaviors of teens who did not (Carter, 2019). Another study found that the rates of STIs did not statistically differ between pledged and non-pledged individuals (Carter, 2019). A 2004 report from Representative Henry Waxman stated that more than 80 percent of the federally funded abstinence-only programs contained false or misleading information about sex (Valenti, 2010). One example of false information in these curricula was found in the abstinence-only curriculum created by *Sex Has a Price Tag* (2003), which was used in schools around America. This curriculum stated that using birth control could kill individuals and that abortion could lead to anorexia and suicide (Valenti, 2010).

According to Anderson (2015), "While noble in intent, the purity movement has resulted in a destructive path of harmful misogyny and exclusion" (p. 22). It left a generation of sexually uninformed and/or misinformed youth confused about their bodies, sex, sexual health, and more. Many Christians were taught a singular ethic from the church—abstinence was required outside of heterosexual marriage; abortion was never acceptable, the use of birth control was discouraged, same-sex relationships were an abomination, and disconnecting one's sex life from one's faith was promoted (McCleneghan, 2011). While processing all of this information, I am curious (by a show of hands) how many of us here participated in an abstinence-only curriculum in their church or school. How many of you received a purity ring or attended a purity culture event?

What were those experiences like for you? Throughout my time as a therapist, I have often been asked about the motivations of purity culture, specifically, "Why did they do this?" and "How did this happen?" While the evangelical church has had a variety of messages specifically targeted at women, one cannot deny that women in the evangelical Christian church were exposed to far-reaching sex-negative messages that were developed by the church as a response to the changing sexual climate and their fear of losing the traditional family.

Evangelical Christians "were concerned with domestic life and the proper execution of the roles of men and women as husbands and wives within the nuclear family" (Fitzgerald, 2017, p. 196). Purity culture described the system of sexual dos and don'ts that were passed down as truths to an entire generation of Christians. Purity culture required complete sexual abstinence until marriage between cisgender, heterosexual, as well as monogamous men and women (Emily J. Allison, 2021). Christians were taught that agape (unconditional) love was the preferred type of love, that philia (friendship) was acceptable, and that eros (erotic love) would lead individuals astray. This insinuated that certain kinds of love were more desirable and acceptable than others (Sellers, 2017). Bromleigh McCleneghan (2011) states that individuals in the evangelical Christian church rarely learned about sexual or romantic love in the context of the church or God. They learned about agape love, but when it came to eros, the church was silent. According to McCleneghan (2011), eros is the desire for another person and the passion that accompanies the desire to express yourself sexually. In essence, eros is vulnerability because it creates the possibility for joy and also for pain. To desire someone else and feel the passion that goes along with that is to be vulnerable. Linda Klein (2018) states that sex became the big issue that marked someone's spiritual standing with God.

Emily J. Allison (2021) writes, "Up until the mid-to-late 1970s, issues related to human sexuality were not a primary aspect of political activism and social organizing for evangelical Christians" (p. 25). In the late nineteenth and early twentieth centuries, the evangelical Christian church, in an attempt to address perceived cultural threats, began disassembling the so-called separation of church and state (which had been a guiding national principle in politics and religious matters) through its political activism, lobbying, and the steady supply of public-school abstinence-only curricula. In addition to these activities, it sought to reinforce these beliefs in churches, youth groups, Christian schools, and religious communities. While the underlying precepts of abstinence-only education in society have not changed significantly in centuries, the development of far-reaching curricula, workshops, books, classroom materials, abstinence pledges, and even purity merchandise have brought about a far more systematic method of delivery for church doctrine. The products evangelical Christians consumed shaped the faith they inhabited, which meant being a conservative evangelical was as much about culture as it was about theology (Kobes Du Mez, 2020). The Abstinence Clearinghouse, which is the largest and most well-known abstinence education nonprofit organization in America, sells abstinence pledge cards on its website and still makes no effort to hide the fact that these cards commodify virginity (Valenti, 2010).

Another product sold by abstinence-only companies was a pin attached to a small card that read "You are like a beautiful rose. Each time you engage in pre-marital sex, a precious petal is stripped away. Don't leave your future husband holding a bare stem. Abstain" (Valenti, 2010, p. 32). The purity movement may have had good intentions, but ultimately became destructive for many. Unfortunately, that destruction was predominantly shouldered by women, leaving a generation of Christian women struggling with unrealistic expectations, disappointment, hurt, sexual dysfunction, and sexual shame.

For adolescent girls who grew up in purity culture, messages of purity and the importance of remaining a virgin until marriage were more than pins and rings. In Dianna Anderson's book *Damaged Goods* (2015), Anderson states that purity proponents believe that sex is a physical, emotional, and spiritually binding act in a heterosexual marriage. In addition, purity means not having sexual or lustful thoughts, that men and women belong to their spouses, and above all, premarital sex is a sin. Materials from this time were especially focused on the preservation of virginity. Jessica Valenti, the author of *The Purity Myth* (2010), explains that "people have been talking authoritatively about virginity for thousands of years, yet we don't even have a working medical definition for it" (p. 20). There is no specific moment when an individual shifts from being a virgin to not being a virgin. Virginity is a social construct, which means it was created by humans. When you have sex (defined by purity culture as a penis penetrating a vagina) for the first time, your identity does not change and it does not affect your value or worth as a person (Smith, 2020). Instead, losing your virginity is a process that happens over time as an individual has more sexual experiences and develops an idea of what sex means to them (Anderson, 2015).

While there is no medical definition for virginity, purity culture often defines virginity as the lack of penile and vaginal penetration. This means that the culture's definition of sex is when a penis penetrates a vagina. This curriculum chooses to define sex as "a journey into an extraordinary state of consciousness, where we tune out everything extraneous to our emotions and our senses in this very moment, travel into a realm of delicious sensation, and soak in the deep connection" (Hardy & Easton, 2017, p. 243). This curriculum defines sex this way because sex is so much more than genital stimulation that may or may not lead to orgasm. Sex that is limited to genitals is an insult to the human body's capacity for pleasure (Hardy & Easton, 2017). Sex outside of marriage was essentially the only "sin" that was said to change someone (Klein, 2018). Another aspect of virginity in purity culture is emotional purity, which is the belief that one can lose purity by becoming emotionally involved with the opposite sex even if physical contact doesn't happen (Anderson, 2015). Girls were routinely taught that their greatest gifts (and what gave them value as Christian women) were their bodies and their "intact" virginity.

Anderson (2015) states that "the purity industry gave many adolescents the impression that sexual abstinence before marriage was the way for them to live out their faith" (p. 23). A woman's worth was found in her ability and willingness to refuse sex because her body and her sexuality were what made her valuable (Valenti, 2010). Female sexuality has been viewed as a commodity and, like all commodities, has more value when it is scarce. This means that a woman who shared her sexuality freely was told she reduced her value (Hardy & Easton, 2017).

In *Virgin Nation: Sexual Purity and American Adolescence* (2015), Sara Moslener, purity culture historian, cites James Dobson, a Christian evangelical author and founder of the conservative Focus on the Family ministry, as describing "'female sexuality as a commodity that reaches the height of its value on the wedding day'" (p. 103). Despite growing up in a culture where young women were exposed to overt sexual messages, they were taught by their parents, teachers, and religious leaders that their only real worth was their virginity and their ability to remain pure (Valenti, 2010). Purity culture endorsed the belief that what mattered most about an individual was whether they had sex in the "right" or "wrong" way. It made wearing a white dress (indicating a pure status) at a woman's wedding a marker of morality (Anderson, 2015).

In addition to a focus on virginity, girls subjected to purity culture were heavily dissuaded from exploring sexual pleasure and/or their bodies. McCleneghan (2011) remarks, "Desire for sexual pleasure among women either did not exist or was a sign of deep confusion about what a true or biblical woman was supposed to be like, was created to be" (p. 20). Girls were often told not to trust themselves or their bodies because their true nature was corrupted by sin. The female body was seen as the root of evil and that it had caused the initial "fall of man" (Finch, 2019, p. 28). Throughout history, Christianity has associated sexual activity with impurity. Augustine argued that original sin was transmitted to every human through sexual intercourse that created new life, which connected sex with sin (Barr, 2021). Although self-exploration and masturbation have had a controversial religious and social history, many professionals and specialists agree that it is a normal and healthy part of sexual development (Davidson, 1984; Davidson & Darling, 1990). Well-known sex therapist Gina Ogden (2008) states,

> Pleasuring yourself can be a crucial part of the journey of self-awareness. You move along at your own pace. It can be a journey of personal wholeness, for pleasuring yourself involves much more than your body. You're involving your mind, emotions, and spirit too. When your involvement is strong, you can forge a sense of sexual partnership with yourself. (p. 54)

The fact that purity culture focused on teenage girls is not an accident. While the rationale of preventing teen pregnancies may have been used by some church leaders, this timing coincides with the development of sexual identity in girls. In fact, the teen years are crucial in the development of one's sexual identity and being. In teenagers who have not suffered sexual trauma, the teen years are typically the time that sexual values, needs, preferred forms of sexual expression, and preferred sexual activities are developed (Muise et al., 2010). Adolescent girls in America experience pressure to be seen and not heard, to be feminine, to suppress their authentic thoughts and feelings, and to conform to the culture's beauty expectations. All of this happens at the same time that they are learning about their bodies and exploring their sexuality (Impett et al., 2006; Tolman, 2002).

Teenage girls were not given a language for sex or sexuality and were ultimately promised incredible sex lives once they got married so long as they remained "pure" before marriage. Jamie Lee Finch (2019) states that "the majority of what comes out of the religious rhetoric is wrapped up in language that describes the physical body, the root of all that is evil, or 'sinful.' Natural human desires are described as ungodly and dangerous and are required to be suppressed until (implied heterosexual) marriage in order to be holy" (p. 31).

These messages deeply affected the sexual development, beliefs, experiences, and self-worth of women for decades to come. The deployment of this modern purity culture has, without a doubt, had long-lasting negative sexual and psychological effects on many of its participants. Beale et al. (2016) found that women in purity culture report significantly higher levels of guilt around sex. In addition, strongly religious women in their study reported greater rates of unsatisfactory sex, higher anxiety levels about that sex, and a prevailing feeling of being incapable of changing their situation. Anderson (2015) states that "evangelical adolescents are also among the least likely to expect sex to be pleasurable, and among the most likely to expect that having sex will make them feel guilty" (p. 27).

Without a doubt, multiple generations have felt the impact of this movement on their sexual beliefs and experiences. We're here to change the internal sexual narrative. That new narrative starts today.

HOMEWORK

You received a lot of information today, which may have been a little overwhelming. My hope is that you leave here today knowing that you are not alone in the experiences that you had in purity culture. I also hope that you feel encouraged that as we continue on this journey together you will find some clarity and healing.

I'd like you all to go home tonight, sit down, and draw your current garden. Think about the messages and seeds that were planted in your garden. Fill your garden drawing with the words, truths, and beliefs you were taught and/or given. The goal is to make a visual representation of your sexual self. Please put your garden somewhere in your home where you can easily see it over the next few weeks as we work together. Feel free to add to your garden as needed. You will be asked to bring the drawing of your garden to our final session together.

DISCUSSION QUESTIONS

- What is your earliest memory of purity culture and its effects on your life?
- Why was this instance so poignant? What made it stick?
- Were/are there any positive impacts of purity culture?
- What are some recollections of sexual education classes you experienced in high school? Were they abstinence-only?
- Were there any pop cultural influences that reinforced the teachings of purity culture in your life?
- Has there been a moment where you felt the evangelical church directly contradicted its own teachings?
- What are some initial plants you'd like to plant in your garden (as described by Emily Nagoski)?
- What are some initial plants you'd like to pull from your garden?

9

✛

Class 2

Shame and Guilt

OBJECTIVES

- Participants will generate a personal definition of shame and guilt.
- Participants will select examples of shame in their life and identify the source.
- Participants will examine personal examples of shame in order to analyze their effects on lifestyle, sexual practices, and sexual self-esteem.

GREETING AND WELCOME

As we discussed in our last session, part of our work in moving past the messages of purity culture is to confront and deconstruct some of the messages we were taught. As we start our class today, I want to begin with an activity that will help you tap into the feeling(s) of shame. I want to ask that during the activity everyone keep their eyes closed so we can all concentrate. This activity may cause an emotional reaction or response, so if you feel that you want to stop, feel free to take a break. I just ask that you keep your eyes closed and allow the other participants to complete the activity.

When you hear the word shame what comes to mind? Where do you feel it in your body? Whose voice pops into your head? What color(s) is it? I want you to think of an experience or a time when you felt shame. Close your eyes and picture that memory. When you can clearly see the situation in your mind, I want you to freeze/pause the memory. Notice how old you are in the memory and who else is in that memory with you. Now I want you to picture your grown-up self stepping into the memory that is frozen. I want you to say or do whatever you want in the memory. When you are done saying and doing what you want, I want you to take the hand of your younger self and walk out of the memory. As you walk out of the memory, I want you to imagine the memory turning to ash and blowing away in the wind. Now, face your younger self and look into her eyes. I want you to tell her what she needs to hear. Once you have told her what she needs to hear, I want you to hug her. Now, open your eyes and come back into the room.

What did that feel like? How do you feel now? Take these next three minutes to write down whatever you experienced so you can take it home and process it later. Shame can only survive in secrecy, so sharing your story or stories of shame can only help you heal. Author, shame researcher, and speaker Brené Brown (2010) states, "Shame hates it when we reach out and tell our story. It hates having words wrapped around it—it can't survive being shared" (p. 10).

GUILT

What is guilt? The Oxford Online Dictionary (2021a) defines guilt as "a feeling of having done wrong or failed in an obligation." Guilt is "feeling badly about doing something specifically wrong or condemning a specific behavior" (Murray et al., 2007, p. 225). Brown (2010) describes guilt as the belief that you did something bad. While shame is ultimately about who we are, guilt is about our behaviors and what we do. We feel guilt when we fail to be the person we want to be. While guilt is as powerful as shame, its effect is typically positive versus destructive like shame's. According to Winell (1993), "Guilt is a signal to do something differently, and this is functional for survival" (p. 185). Guilt often motivates people to change behaviors, apologize, and make amends. Shame, on the other hand, breaks down the part of us that believes we can change or do differently (Brown, 2010).

The neurotic guilt that is often fostered in religion tends to be excessive and inappropriate. It is based on the expectations of others instead of on your own personal values. It focuses on the mistake instead of using the guilty feelings to make a change (Winell, 1993). Guilt can seep into our lives when we do not follow the rules of our church, family, culture, etc. When an individual realizes they have violated an ethical, moral, or religious principle, it can create feelings of guilt, which in turn decreases self-esteem. Purity culture had a lot of rules around sexuality and modesty for women, which created guilt for some individuals who chose not to follow those rules or found themselves in situations where the rules couldn't be followed. Individuals who feel guilt about their sexual behaviors often experience sex guilt that may be socially and religiously constructed (Davidson et al., 2004).

Sex guilt has been defined as "a generalized expectancy for self-mediated punishment for violating or anticipating violating standards for proper sexual conduct" (Murray et al., 2007, p. 222). A study by Ogren (1974) found that sex guilt from religious training and experiences affected sexual attitudes and behaviors. A study conducted by Fox and Young (1989) found that women who had high levels of religiosity had higher levels of sex guilt as well. This may lead one to believe that exposure to certain religious teachings could inhibit sexual expression due to guilt (Murray et al., 2007). Traditionally, religion separated sexuality between the body and the spirit, which is known as a dualistic split. There was a tendency to control the sexual expression of religious followers, particularly outside of marriage (Murray et al., 2007). More recently, religion has been emphasizing more of a connection between spirituality and sexual expression, even though traditional beliefs and practices, as well as biblical texts, were used to keep traditional sexual values in place by creating a sense of moral superiority (McClintock, 2001).

SHAME

What is shame? The Oxford Online Dictionary (2021b) defines shame as "a painful feeling of humiliation or distress caused by the consciousness of wrong or foolish behavior." Brown (2013) defines shame as "an intensely painful feeling or experience of believing that we are flawed and therefore unworthy of love and belonging" (para. 2). Matthias Roberts (2020) defines shame as "the fear of disconnection. It is the voices both inside and outside of us that convince us we are not worthy of connection because of who we are or what we have done" (p. 170). Rosemary Mills (2004) defines shame as "an experience of attribution about the whole self. It is an intense, negative feeling about the self in its entirety" (p. 30). While these are just a few definitions of shame, I am sure you could each write your own definition based on your experiences with shame. Is there a specific definition of shame that resonates with you? If so, would anyone like to share?

Finding a consistent definition of shame is difficult because in the English language there is only one word that is used to describe the feeling of shame. Other languages have one word that describes internal shame and an entirely different word that describes shame toward an individual and/or group (McClintock, 2001). Shame is known as "the master emotion" (Brown, 2010, p. 40) because we don't have to experience it to be paralyzed by it; the fear of being perceived as unworthy is enough to silence our experiences and stories. Shame is something everyone experiences (Brown, 2010; Sznycer et al., 2012), and it needs three things to grow: secrecy, silence, and judgment. While we may assume that shame is found in the darkest areas of life, it is often found in the familiar parts of our lives. Places like our family, religion, place of employment, thoughts, and attitudes about ourselves, and even sex (Brown, 2010).

How do people deal with shame? Some individuals deal with shame by allowing it to take control, which Roberts (2020) calls "shamefulness" (p. 19). Shamefulness is based on the belief that there is a right context for sexual expression and a wrong context for sexual expression. We feel shameful when our sexual interests, our gender identity, or our fantasies do not fit into what others consider to be the right box (Roberts, 2020). Purity culture was a culture where sex was surrounded by right and wrong, which created internalized shame. Purity culture taught that having sex outside of marriage was wrong and since people didn't want to be "bad" or "wrong," they avoided all things sexual. Individuals worked hard to control their thoughts and the media they consumed. Individuals tried to control their shame by controlling their sexuality and in instances where they couldn't, they hid. When this happens, we come up with ways to eradicate and/or avoid the parts of our sexuality that fall into the "wrong" box. Sometimes this works, but more often than not we fall off the wagon or make a mistake, which creates more shame (Roberts, 2020).

The other way that people can deal with shame is shamelessness. In choosing shamelessness, you cannot escape from shame. Instead, we choose to believe we are shameless. In choosing shamelessness you can either acknowledge and welcome the shame and learn to use it, or you can create ways to protect yourself from it. We attempt to ignore the shame while never being able to completely escape from it. Shamelessness can easily be misrepresented for sex positivity, where anything and everything is OK and where an individual disregards their core values to avoid feeling shame (Roberts, 2020). Roberts (2020) states, "Instead of hiding from our shame, we stare it in the eyes, and say, 'I'm simply not going to feel you anymore.' We push shame aside or into a corner within ourselves, and then we proceed with our fun" (p. 34).

For individuals who grew up within purity culture, shamelessness can often go hand in hand with deconstruction because if following God means living inside the strict boxes of shame, leaving God and/or your faith sounds a lot better. Unfortunately, ignoring shame does not make it go away; instead, it begins to seep in. According to Roberts (2020), "Only after we've stopped avoiding our shame can we truly work through it. Our behaviors and actions may not actually change that much. But instead of acting from a place of defensiveness, instead of working to convince ourselves and everyone around us that we're free of shame, we're operating from a place of grounding" (p. 38).

So how do you face your shame? The first step is acknowledging that it exists and welcoming it. We often want to push shame away or avoid thinking about it because it is painful. But it is when we acknowledge and welcome the shame without judgment that we are able to move through it. Notice where the shame is held in your body. Notice if there is a color or specific feeling or word associated with it. If there is a specific place that it is held in your body, intentionally focus on that body part and breathe into it with a calming color or word. Listen to what that body part may need to tell you. The goal is not to erase or change the shame, but to feel it and move through it. As you breathe out, visualize the shame leaving that part of the body. Simply bringing your attention to the shame can often move the shame.

DISCUSSION QUESTIONS

- What is your earliest memory of shame? What made it so memorable?
- At what age did you feel ashamed? What were the sources of that shame?
- Do you currently feel shame for anything in your life? What does that look like? Is there something that triggers that shame?
- Are there things in your life that you don't do because of the anticipation of shame? Where did the messaging come from that told you that activity was shameful?

HOMEWORK

I would like you all to go home tonight and have a hot shower. As you watch and feel the water flow down your body, I want you to think about the shame you may have felt during your life. Notice where you are holding that shame in your body. Notice if it has a color, a scent, a taste, or a specific sound associated with it. As the water from the shower hits your body, I want you to visualize the shame that is being held in your body slowly leaving your body with the water that is going down the drain. You may notice that you are not ready to let go of all of your shame and that is OK. Don't judge yourself, but instead be curious about where that shame is being held and why it is not ready to be released. As you exit the shower and dry off, I want you to thank your body for all it has done for you over your life. Allow yourself to embrace your body as it moves forward, feeling a little bit lighter after letting go of some of the shame it has been carrying around.

10

✝

Class 3

Religious Shame Around Sexuality

OBJECTIVES

- Participants will generate a personal definition of sexual shame.
- Participants will select examples of sexual shame in their life and identify the source.
- Participants will examine personal examples of sexual shame to analyze their effects on lifestyle, sexual practices, and sexual self-esteem.

GREETING AND WELCOME

I want to start out with a poignant quote from Linda Klein: "The purity message is not about sex. Rather, it's about us: who we are, who we are expected to be, and who it is said we will become if we fail to meet those expectations. This is the language of shame" (as cited in Emily Allison, 2021, pp. 36–37). As we begin the session, I'd like to do an activity that will help you identify some of the messages you received as part of purity culture and the potential shame they solicited. Let's take a look at examples of these messages. Some might look familiar while others might not. We'll still take a minute to review what each says to the viewer. (Participants will view a slideshow of terms/messages from purity culture.)

Shame is a well-researched topic and is supported by various scientific measures. However, researchers admit that research on sexual shame is lacking. In fact, most of the research on sexual shame has occurred only in the past twenty years. Researchers have steered clear of sexual shame research and measures due to the perceived taboo status of sexual shame. Jeffrey Weeks (1989) states that "the erotic still arouses acute moral anxiety and confusion. This is not because sex is intrinsically 'naughty,' but because it is a focus for powerful feelings" (p. 18).

Sex brings up emotion(s) when it is discussed, which can make it a difficult topic to research because the researchers involved could potentially show bias based on their life experiences and/or beliefs. Using Brené Brown's definition of shame as the basis for creating a definition of sexual shame, one could define sexual shame as an intensely painful feeling or experience resulting in the belief that we are flawed and therefore unworthy of acceptance and belonging due to our sexual thoughts, experiences, or behaviors. Sexual shame has also been defined as "the emotional experience of unworthiness" (Murray et al., 2007, p. 225) that revolves around events from the past. It can involve aspects of sexuality that are generally unchangeable such as attraction and gender (McClintock, 2001).

Paraphrasing findings from Coleman (2002), Hungrige (2016) remarks, "Shame related to sexuality is a very common experience for many individuals due to the belief that they are digressing from society's accepted standard" (p. 57). Individuals are often very young when they are introduced to sexual shame, whether through sexual secrecy, sexual abuse, exposure to pornography, religious shaming, being dressed to hide the body, or being shamed for masturbation or promiscuity (Hastings, 1998). Often, the greatest shaming of an individual occurs during the vulnerable time of learning about sexuality. Sexual shame begins with rules that require someone to abstain from any talk about sex, and individuals have sexual issues and problems transferred to them from previous generations. This cycle of not discussing anything related to sex and passing down family secrets produces unspoken shame (McClintock, 2001).

A number of research studies have found a link between sex guilt, sexual behavior, sexual attitudes, and religiosity (McClintock, 2001; Tangney & Dearing, 2003). It's hard to research shame and sexual shame without running across religion and the effects it has had on the feelings, beliefs, and shame individuals carry with them throughout life. Shaming is often common in religious communities because it is intertwined with core beliefs, theology, and doctrine, making it difficult to see (Anderson, 2015). Hardy and Easton (2017) state, "Believing that God doesn't like sex is like believing that God doesn't like you" (p. 13). When individuals are given this message, they tend to carry around shame for completely natural sexual desires and feelings (Hardy & Easton, 2017). Therapist Tina Sellers (2017) writes, "When a religious, sexual component is added to an experience of condemnation, it becomes religious sexual shame, which only amplifies the shame impact" (p. xxv).

Women, in particular, have carried around religious sexual shame for centuries due to the teachings of Christianity. Reporting results from Fox and Young (1989), Klein (2018) notes that girls are 92 percent more likely to experience sexual guilt than boys (p. 27). Females reported significantly higher sex guilt than males and sex guilt from the first sexual experience is predictive of higher sex anxiety, lower sexual efficacy, and lower sexual satisfaction. Therefore, women who have strong religious beliefs and have engaged in premarital sex have had unsatisfactory sex, have high anxiety about it, and do not feel that they are capable of changing their situation. Lastly, Fox and Young also found that "the relationship between sex and guilt, sex anxiety, sexual efficacy, and sexual satisfaction, doesn't diminish over time; it gets stronger" (Klein, 2018, p. 28).

In the evangelical Christian community, women were often described as the gatekeepers to sexuality. Women were told that they were less sexual than men and were, therefore, the gatekeepers of sexual morals within the community (Anderson, 2015). They were expected to keep men from engaging in lustful or sexual thoughts and/or behaviors. Purity culture routinely shamed girls for normal sexual expression. This shame followed them into adulthood, causing disturbances in relationships, intimacy, libido, and sexuality. Sexual shame can interfere with pleasure because it affects a person's ability to feel seen, known, loved, and accepted with and through their sensual self (Sellers, 2017). These girls grew up in a world where they often felt shame about their bodies, their libido, and all things sex-related. They weren't taught to ask why God might have given them their desires for sexual intimacy, what it might say about God's character that God invented sex, or even how men and women are wired differently as sexual creatures (Sellers, 2017). Instead, they were given the message that pursuing their pleasure would lead them away from God and that giving in to lust and/or fantasy would result in addiction (McCleneghan, 2011).

St. Paul the apostle even described women to be sexual temptresses and strongly disapproved of any form of sexual activity that focused on sexual pleasure (Boswell, 1980; Davidson et al., 1995). Paul's writings were confusing when it came to spirituality and sexuality because he preached that love of God and human sexual love were not compatible. During the time of Paul, the religious leaders taught that holiness required suppression of sexual desires in order to pursue a life of faith (McClintock, 2001). When sexuality was discussed in evangelical church settings, the conversation was often focused on the concept of purity, especially when it came to women (Beck, 2006). Anderson (2015) states that in the evangelical community, an "impure" girl or woman wasn't just seen as damaged; she was considered dangerous. She was dangerous to the men and the community because if the male leaders fell, everything in the community would crumble. Women felt the pressure to remain pure and virginal in order to give themselves value while also feeling responsible for keeping men pure.

The purity movement addressed lust and modesty in such a way that women were made to feel responsible for how men behaved. Women were expected to wear modest clothing in order to keep men from "stumbling." This taught women to distrust men and taught men that they were not responsible for their behavior or sexual desire(s). This made women see their own sexual desires and bodies as dangerous, causing many of them to bury their sexual feelings (Sellers, 2017). People in the evangelical church associated modesty exclusively with women and their need to protect themselves from men and from unintentionally seducing men. This was a form of social control (McCleneghan, 2011). Michael Bader (2002) states that shame, rejection, and helplessness extinguish sexual desire.

Emily Allison, author of #*Churchtoo* (2021), states that each individual community defines what modesty looks like, which creates a sense of guilt for women who do not comply or meet the modesty standards. Some Christians find themselves unable to bring their sexuality out into the open when they do get married because they struggle to see it as a good, God-given thing after so many years of shaming themselves for having natural erotic thoughts and feelings (Sellers, 2017). These healthy and natural feelings and/or desires that are part of the human experience were painted in a light that insinuated they were unnatural or bad. The church has been in the business of shaming individuals for seeking pleasure for a very long time (McCleneghan, 2011). Women are left feeling confused and alone in their experiences despite the fact that "one-third of U.S. women, ages 20–44, are single, and 9 out of 10 of them have had sex" (Valenti, 2010, p. 58).

In purity culture, the focus is on pleasing the male partner, but female pleasure is rarely addressed. In purity culture, women were told that they could only discover sexuality in the context of being pursued by a man. Sexual feelings they had could only be expressed in marriage, with the approval and guidance of their husband. The idea that women could desire sex for pleasure was rarely discussed (Roberts, 2020).

Being told that you would have amazing sex if you saved yourself for marriage was not only untrue but gave women completely unrealistic expectations. Anderson (2015) states that the bond of marriage does not make the act of sex unitive. The church talked about modesty and purity but not about the importance of sexual desire, pleasure, consent, or satisfaction. Emily J. Allison (2021) states that pleasure experienced and savored is the antidote for shame. The church often created an environment that encouraged silence around sex, which made it even more difficult for women to communicate their feelings and questions when it came to sex and sexuality.

Sellers (2017) has found in her research that around 80 percent of people raised in the United States grew up in homes that were silent, ignorant, or reactive about sexuality and sexual development. It is not a far reach to assume that this percentage would be even higher in religious homes. Paul Gilbert (2003) explored the differences between internal versus external shame, where external shame is concerned with the evaluation of others while internal shame is related to internal self-judgment. Gilbert notes that internal shame goes past self-criticism and enters an area of hostility toward the self. When women feel hostility toward themselves, they often feel powerless or worthless, which in turn makes them seclude themselves from others and push others away. Psychologist Colleen Conklin (2019) states that "when an internal shame reaction is deeply embedded within a person, self-compassion is a stark deviation from one's natural response" (p. 3).

There is also a correlation between sexual shame and alienation from God, which indicates that individuals experiencing sexual shame may believe that God has abandoned or punished them for their actions or thoughts (Marcinechová & Záhorcová, 2020). Emily J. Allison (2021) paraphrases a conversation she had with Sellers summarizing the impact of sexual shame, writing that Sellers told her, "I don't think there is a greater way that you can hurt people than sexual shame. . . . And it is why sexual shame looks so much like sexual abuse, because it is sexual abuse" (p. 62).

Sellers (2017) also states that when working with Christian clients who have experienced religious sexual shame, it is imperative that we help them "see their belovedness and begin to live into a sex-positive Gospel ethic, one in which they feel seen, known, loved, and accepted while they seek to see, know, love, and accept another" (p. 99). Anderson (2015) states,

> God doesn't function in a currency of shame. Shame isn't from God, it isn't of God, and it isn't something Christians should engage in. Shame is not nor will it ever be a useful response to a person's experience of the world, especially when it comes to sexual experiences. Whatever you have done, whatever has happened to you, whatever people have told you: shame is not the answer. You are worthy of love, you are worthy of grace, and you have no reason to be ashamed. (p. 187)

Helping women identify and process the shame they have carried from exposure to religious teachings and beliefs is imperative since certain religious beliefs and feelings can stifle people's sexual expression to the point that they can incur significant emotional distress (Murray et al., 2007). Going from a sex-negative frame of mind to a sex-positive one enables women to experience healthy and pleasurable sex. Helping women combine new sexual ethics and beliefs with their faith can be life changing. Anderson (2015) describes healthy sexuality as:

> One that takes others into account, that asks for maturity and understanding and respects others and their bodies. . . . It does not place sex on a pedestal, allowing it to overpower a person's life, or let it take unnecessary precedence over one's spiritual life. (p. 40)

Religious sexual shame can affect many areas of a woman's life. Helping women identify and deconstruct this shame and replace it with confidence in themselves as women and as sexual beings will change not only their lives but also the entire culture moving forward. According to Roberts (2020), "If shame is the fear of disconnection, the way we work with our own shame is by embracing connection" (p. 171). In fact, Roberts argues, "As shame is embraced, it begins to lose its power. We begin to see ourselves more clearly, with new eyes. We begin to see how radiant we actually are" (p. 175).

DISCUSSION QUESTIONS

- What is your earliest memory of sexual shame? What made it so memorable?
- At what age did you feel sexually ashamed? What were the sources of that shame?
- Do you currently feel sexual shame for anything in your life? What does that look like? Is there something that triggers that shame?
- Are there sexual activities you don't do because of the anticipation of sexual shame? Where did the messaging come from that told you that activity was shameful?

HOMEWORK

I'd like you all to go home tonight and do something that relaxes you. You could go for a walk, take a bath, journal, or snuggle your pet. Since we will focus on reclaiming your sexuality over the next few weeks, I want you to come up with three words that you would like to focus on. These three words will become your mantra. An example of a sex-positive mantra is *I am sensual. I am sexy. My arousal is beautiful.* Please write down your mantra and say it to yourself each morning before you start your day and each night before you go to bed.

11

✛

Class 4

Sexual Ethics

OBJECTIVES

- Participants will identify their current sexual ethics and the sources of these ethics.
- Participants will define sexual terminology that will aid in their understanding of sexual ethics concepts.
- Participants will deconstruct the various elements of complementarianism.
- Participants will compare and contrast the definitions of gender vs. sexuality.

GREETING AND WELCOME

Before we get into the primary focus of today's session, let's take some time to unpack some of the terms you'll see and hear today. While some individuals question the usefulness of a plethora of terms used to describe gender and sexuality, I accept and support this constantly changing landscape. While the new and ever-changing terms may be overwhelming, I think we have to celebrate the cause of the quick changes. We are, as a society, finally writing down the words to describe (and validate) what has been unspoken for millennia. The excitement at this gradual acceptance of alternative terminology is commendable. But it does occasionally result in confusion as the language evolves. We'll do a quick overview of some of the important terms that will come up later in our discussion.

Cisgender—Someone who exclusively identifies as their sex assigned at birth. The term cisgender is not indicative of gender expression, sexual orientation, hormonal makeup, physical anatomy, or how one is perceived in daily life.

Heterosexual—Someone who is sexually attracted to people of the opposite sex.

Gender Identity—One's internal sense of being male, female, neither of these, both, or other gender(s). *Everyone has a gender identity, including you.* For transgender people, their sex assigned at birth and their gender identity are not necessarily the same.

Gender Expression/Presentation—The physical manifestation of one's gender identity through clothing, hairstyle, voice, body shape, etc. (typically referred to as masculine or feminine). Many transgender people seek to make their gender expression (how they look) match their gender identity (who they are), rather than their sex assigned at birth. Someone with a gender-nonconforming gender expression may or may not be transgender.

Queer—A term for people of marginalized gender identities and sexual orientations who are not cisgender and/or heterosexual. This term has a complicated history as a reclaimed slur.

Sexual Orientation—A person's physical, romantic, emotional, aesthetic, and/or other form of attraction to others. In Western cultures, gender identity and sexual orientation are not the same. Trans people can be straight, bisexual, lesbian, gay, asexual, pansexual, queer, etc. just like anyone else. For example, a trans woman who is exclusively attracted to other women would often identify as lesbian.

LGBTQIAPP+—A collection of identities short for lesbian, gay, bisexual, trans, queer, questioning, intersex, asexual, aromantic, pansexual, polysexual (sometimes abbreviated to LGBT or LGBTQ+). Sometimes this acronym is replaced with "queer." Note that "ally" is not included in this acronym (Definitions, n.d.).

Purity culture assumed that everyone was cisgender, that everyone identified with the gender that they were assigned to at birth, and that everyone was heterosexual. Purity culture assumed that all men and women acted the same and desired the same things. There was strict enforcement of gender roles that created a culture where men and women were cautious of one another (Anderson, 2015). Men were told that they were "sex fiends," not emotional, and could be deceptive. Men were taught to distrust their feelings and that lust was an expected part of being masculine. This reinforced that women were the gatekeepers of sexuality and taught women that men could not be trusted (Klein, 2018). According to Kobes Du Mez (2020), "To be a man was to have a fragile ego and a vigorous libido. Men were entitled to lead, to rule, and to have their needs met—all their needs, on their terms" (p. 64).

Conversely, men were taught that they were the leaders at home, work, and church. Men were encouraged to make financial decisions for their wives and families. Fatherhood was highly valued, and men were expected to be able to financially support their families while their wives were encouraged to be stay-at-home mothers (Bahr & Chadwick, 1985). Men were taught that it is natural for them to be sexually aggressive and that they should be the sexual initiators while the women were taught to be passive responders and withholders. In a study conducted by Gregoire et al. (2021) among evangelical women, it was found that 81.2 percent believed that boys would want to push the sexual boundaries of girls. Therefore, girls needed to adopt the job of sexual gatekeeper to protect their purity. Men got the message to be pushy and women got the message that anything other than the answer "no" made them slutty. This created a pattern where "no" was heard as an invitation for men to push harder, which often resulted in abuse (Hardy & Easton, 2017). Some women felt trapped by the financial dynamic in which men held most of the financial power. Women felt trapped because they didn't have access to money since they were stay-at-home mothers whose finances were controlled by their husbands. Women were expected to be helpers to their husbands, raise the children, and be submissive. A woman was taught that her highest calling was to enhance the life of her husband and children. Women were taught to practice selflessness and obedience. Women were taught to suppress their personal desires and dreams for the sake of their families (Barr, 2021).

Women were viewed as the guardians of religion and morality in the family and community (Bahr & Chadwick, 1985). Being a wife and mother gave evangelical women value and credibility in the community. They were called to secondary roles in church and family with the main emphasis on being a wife and a mother (Barr, 2021). Purity culture taught that men were producers of knowledge while women were consumers of knowledge (Roberts, 2020). This is also known as complementarianism, which is the theology that says men and women have different roles that are not interchangeable despite the belief that God created men and women as equals. Men are made to lead while women are made to follow. Men are initiators while women are expected to accept (Emily Allison, 2021). Barr (2021) defines complementarianism as "the theological view that women are divinely created as helpers and men are divinely created as leaders" (p. 5). According to Barr, complementarianism rewards women who follow the rules. Women who keep silent ensure their husbands remain the leaders, women who keep silent can exercise influence in the community, women who keep silent can maintain friendship and trust with the women in their community, and women who remain silent can ultimately maintain a comfortable life. Christians who have remained silent have allowed misogyny and abuse to grow in the church and many evangelical teachings oppress women. Complementarian theology claims to defend a natural interpretation of the Bible while in reality, it defends an interpretation that has been corrupted by the desire to dominate others and build hierarchies of power and oppression, which is the complete opposite of being Christlike. Barr (2021) states, "The greatest trick the devil ever pulled was convincing Christians that oppression is godly" (p. 173). In evangelical Christianity, men are viewed as "strong, decisive, and straightforward while women are soft, compliant, and strategic" (Emily Allison, 2021, p. 147). This gender divide implies that there are only two genders—cisgender men and women—and that anyone outside of this framework is not welcome in complementarianism (Allison, 2021).

Complementarianism believes that sexual deviancy is inevitable when we fail to follow God's plan for sex and gender. This is of course based on the complementarian interpretation of what the Bible says (Emily Allison, 2021). Barr (2021) notes, "Conservative evangelicals believed that the key to reducing sexual temptation for men was emphasizing purity for women" (p. 156). Women were taught that they could only explore sexuality when being pursued by a man. Sexual feelings could only be expressed in marriage as long as the husband approved and was able to guide the experience (Roberts, 2020). The teachings of the evangelical Christian church oppressed women by fighting to control their bodies from their "natural" fallenness despite the fact that Jesus always fought to set women free (Barr, 2021). Anderson (2015) writes,

> Purity culture states that sex is the binding act of marriage; marriage is God-created and between one man and one woman for all time; that purity means no sexual thoughts of lust; that men and women belong—physically, metaphysically, emotionally, spiritually—to their spouses; and that the Bible clearly says that premarital sex is a sin. (p. 24)

In purity culture, sex is mysterious, rarely discussed, and reserved solely for heterosexual marriage (Roberts, 2020). Tim and Beverly LaHaye published a guide to marriage in 1968 called *How to Be Happy Though Married* (2009) that promoted "male headship," which is the belief that men have authority over their wives and are responsible for their protection. While the LaHayes were not anti-sex, they felt it was important to offer a more biblical model of sexual liberation; that is, as Kobes Du Mez (2020) paraphrases, "the liberation of heterosexual couples to freely enjoy sex within the confines of patriarchal marriage" (p. 91). The LaHayes promoted the belief that God designed man to be the aggressor, provider, and leader of his family, and that these roles were directly connected to a man's sex drive. In order to be an aggressive male leader, you had to have an aggressive sex drive. It was the responsibility of women to sexually satisfy their husbands because this stroked their ego, which in turn made them better leaders. If a husband lacked confidence, his wife was encouraged to "make aggressive love to him . . . [and] dress provocatively and use feminine charm to seduce him" (Kobes Du Mez, 2020, p. 91). Books on marriage written by Christian authors of the time told women that even when their emotional, physical, or safety needs were not being met, having sex with their husbands could fix their problems (Gregoire et al., 2021). According to the LaHayes, a wife's failure in the bedroom would undoubtedly have consequences and if a man didn't enjoy the way his wife had sex with him, he would find ways to make his disapproval known. Women were also taught that if they were not sexually available to their husbands in the ways that the Song of Songs described, their husbands may find themselves trapped in infidelity. And while the wife might not be responsible for her husband's sin, she certainly wasn't helping him (Kobes Du Mez, 2020). Kobes Du Mez (2020) describes how "wives were tasked with meeting husbands' every sexual need, but it was the responsibility of women and girls to avoid leading men who were not their husbands into temptation" (p. 170).

In 1977, James Dobson founded Focus on the Family, which was a parachurch organization dedicated to defending the institution of the family. Dobson focused a lot on upholding traditional family values. Unfortunately, family values politics was never really about protecting the well-being of American families. Instead, so-called evangelical family values reinforced patriarchal authority and were really about sex and power (Kobes Du Mez, 2020). In fact, "By the end of the 1970s, the defense of patriarchal power had emerged as an evangelical distinctive" (Kobes Du Mez, 2020, p. 12). In 1975, Dobson took it upon himself to focus on the preservation of distinct gender roles. Quoting from Dobson's *What Wives Wish Their Husbands Knew About Women* (1975), Kobes Du Mez (2020) writes that Dobson believed that there were distinct differences in males and females "biochemically, anatomically, and emotionally" (p. 82). According to Dobson, men liked to "hunt and fish and hike in the wilderness" while women preferred to "stay at home and wait for them" (as cited in Kobes Du Mez, 2020, p. 82). The biggest difference between men and women, according to Dobson, was their source of self-esteem. More specifically, Dobson (1975) wrote, "Men derived self-esteem by being respected; women felt worthy when they were loved" (as cited in Kobes Du Mez, 2020, p. 83). What Dobson taught about women was not biblical. Instead, it was rooted in the cult of domesticity and ancient ideas about the biological inferiority of women. Dobson was preaching the nineteenth-century cult of domesticity (Barr, 2021). According to historian Randall Balmer, evangelicals have failed to realize that the "traditional concept of femininity that we believe to be from the Bible is nothing more than a 'nineteenth-century construct'" (Barr, 2021, p. 171). Dobson (1975) believed there needed to be distinct gender roles and identities for the sake of marriage and also for the sake of the nation. Dobson noted that "we must not abandon the Biblical concept of masculinity and femininity at this delicate stage of our national history" (as cited in Kobes Du Mez, 2020, p. 83). Two decades later, in 1994, Dobson wrote about why men should be the sole breadwinners:

> I wish it were possible for me to emphasize just how critical this masculine understanding is to family stability. . . . One of the greatest threats to the institution of the family today is the undermining of this role as protector and provider. This is the contribution for which men were designed. . . . If it is taken away, their commitment to their wives and children is jeopardized. (as cited in Barr, 2021, pp. 30–31)

Dobson believed that the nation would remain strong and stable if we stuck to traditional masculine and feminine roles. By the mid-1980s, Dobson's half-hour radio show was playing on nearly 800 stations across America (Kobes Du Mez, 2020).

Marriage is an exclusively heterosexual, cisgender institution that ignores a large part of the population that does not fall into these boxes (Anderson, 2015). This means that members of the LGBTQIA+ community were often ignored and/or ostracized for being different. Queer sexuality was rarely discussed in churches, youth groups, or abstinence-only programs (Valenti, 2010). As Gina Ogden (2008) states, "The law of the land says that sex is supposed to happen between couples, preferably male and female" (p. 51). It is a well-known fact that sex between same-sex couples and people with differing gender identities was considered sinful and often shamed. According to Kobes Du Mez (2020), "Same-sex relationships challenged the most basic assumptions of the evangelical worldview" (p. 63). Being a part of the LGBTQI+ community was often viewed by the evangelical church as being a choice, one that you could reject if you had enough self-control (Erika Allison, 2021).

It is important to remember that sexuality is fluid, which means an individual's sexuality can change over time and we need to meet people where they are instead of trying to change them into what we believe they should be (Anderson, 2015). Gender and sexual orientation are also fluid. Some Christians make a distinction between sexuality and sex, which has enabled them to attack members of the LGBTQIA+ community by enforcing celibacy and trying to regulate who is allowed to have sex and who is not and in what contexts (Roberts, 2020).

Exodus International, an ex-gay organization created in the mid-1970s, maintained the belief that gay men and lesbians could change their sexual orientation through prayer and psychotherapy. They used conversion or restorative therapy to enforce celibacy among the LGBTQIA+ community and their focus was on changing the sexual orientation of same-sex-attracted people. They believed that the only healthy and/or acceptable sexual identity was heterosexuality. More than 700,000 people received conversion therapy, half of whom were under the age of 18 (Erika Allison, 2021). Conversion therapy was not only abusive and traumatic, but there is no sound research that indicates that a person's sexual orientation can be changed. Ex-gay organizations implied that sexuality could be changed, and gender could be trained. The problem with this logic is that if you can train someone to move their sexuality or gender in one direction then they should be able to do the same in the opposite direction (Gerber, 2008). After much of the damage was already done, president Alan Chambers wrote a letter in 2013 prior to the organization closing its doors, stating,

> I am sorry for the pain and hurt many of you have experienced. . . . I am sorry that some of you spent years working through the shame and guilt you felt when your attractions didn't change. I am sorry we promoted sexual orientation change efforts and reparative theories about sexual orientation that stigmatized parents. (As cited in Lovett, 2013)

Anderson (2015) states, "Purity culture creates an 'ethic' in which the only guiding principle is 'no'" (p. 145). It consists of a set of rules about when to say no instead of teaching individuals how to say yes. Instead of focusing on waiting for marriage to have sex, the church should have focused on waiting until you were ready to have sex (Anderson, 2015). Now that you no longer live in that world, you get to decide what your sexual ethics are. You get to reflect on all of the messages you were given and keep what works for you, while letting go of everything that no longer serves you.

You may find that the values that have determined your sexual choices are ones you still agree with, are proud of, and want to keep. You may find that some of your sexual choices have come from values you no longer hold, values that helped you cope with the trauma you experienced but no longer help you live the way you want to (Erika Allison, 2021). Developing your own sexual ethics will allow you to own your body and your sexuality (Anderson, 2015). Adopting a sexual ethic that takes others into account requires maturity, consent, and respect for others.

Whether inside or outside of marriage, sexual ethics do not place sex on a pedestal or allow it to take over someone's life. A healthy sexual ethic is one that focuses on honoring yourself and others, loving fully, and exercising restraint or indulgence when appropriate (Anderson, 2015). Sexual ethics enable you to make yourself an active participant in your sexual life instead of being someone to whom experiences randomly happen, allowing yourself to acknowledge what you want instead of what you think you should want or have been told to want (Erika Allison, 2021). When creating your own sexual ethics, Anderson (2015) suggests taking these points into consideration:

1. sexuality has many facets;
2. your body belongs to you and no one else;
3. you need to understand how your body works;
4. sexual activity should be pleasurable and consensual; and
5. sexuality is fluid and complex.

(Erika Allison, 2021, p. 54)

Meanwhile, Nagoski (2015a) argues that "how you feel about your sexuality is more important than your sexuality" (p. 295). When creating your own sexual ethics, consider incorporating some of these truths: that pleasure is safe and appropriate; that eroticism won't get out of control or become destructive; that you can connect with someone without being exploited; and that you can trust your partner when they express their desire, arousal, or satisfaction (Klein, 2012).

SEXUAL INTELLIGENCE

Sex therapist Marty Klein (2012) defines sexual intelligence as "dealing with sexuality in a straightforward way, rather than hiding it, denying it, or blaming it" (p. 27). Sexual intelligence is your ability to relax, be present, communicate, respond to stimulation, and create physical and emotional connections with other people. Sexual intelligence is your ability to create and maintain desire during an uncomfortable situation; it is the ability to adapt to unforeseen changes in your life and in your body; it is being curious about what pleasure is; it is connection and satisfaction; and it is the ability to adapt when something doesn't go as planned (Klein, 2012). For example, you or your partner might burp during sex, get a cramp while having sex, or lose an erection. According to Klein (2012), "The three components of sexual intelligence are information and knowledge, emotional skills (which let you use that knowledge), and body awareness and comfort (which let you express yourself and your knowledge" (p. 55).

This type of knowledge is getting the information you need about your body and your partner's body. Learning what your preferences (and your partner's preferences) are when it comes to what you/they find erotic, desirable, and what potential barriers (such as health problems) may come into play. Sexual intelligence is a narrative of personal adequacy, of presence, of connection, of sufficiency, of agency and ownership of your own body, of relaxation, and of acceptance. Sexual intelligence is allowing yourself not to care about or focus on what isn't important, and instead identifying and focusing on what is important to you (Klein, 2012). Klein (2012) argues that improving your sexual intelligence is the most reliable way to enhance your sexual experience.

Evangelical Christianity claimed that its values and judgments around sex and sexuality were dictated by God even though they were subjective and created by humans with human biases (Klein, 2012). When a person or group of people claim to know what's sexually "normal," it creates a power dynamic that undermines intimacy (Klein, 2012). Purity culture judged its members against a standard of what they claimed to be sexually "normal" and/or acceptable. This belief diminished the individuality of its members and encouraged them to conform to the values of purity culture out of fear of being "other," sinning, or not belonging.

The feeling of being "other" isn't erased once you leave purity culture, but once you step outside of or away from purity culture, you become "other." What are your thoughts on being "other"? How would/does that feel? Is it scary to step into this world of "other"? Purity culture focused so much on getting everyone to conform that going a different way became the quickest way to end up alone. If we think that sex has inherent meaning and that it's our job to conform to that meaning, we will be unable to view sex from a fresh perspective and will accept the erotic limits imposed on us by the church (Klein, 2012).

Organized religion is often controlling and limits people's sexual expression by claiming to know what sex "means" or what its "purpose" is. This is an attempt to control its followers by requiring them to adapt their sexual expression to the values and morals of the church. People are afraid that if they do not conform to the church's inherent meaning of sex, they will behave unethically. They believe it's the role of religion to control the behavior of followers and that the lack of religion results in the removal of ethical regulation. Embracing sexual intelligence allows an individual to own their sexuality instead of serving it. It gives an individual the freedom to enjoy sex the way they want to instead of being bound to the need of fulfilling a sexual narrative created by someone else (Klein, 2012).

DISCUSSION

- How would you define your current sexual ethics?
- What were the sources of these ethics?
- Were there any sexual ethics terms that surprised you?

- What is your view of gender vs. sexuality? Has this viewpoint changed recently? If so, what has affected that change?
- Now that you're aware of the concept of sexual intelligence, do you anticipate changes in how you view sex? Do you anticipate changes in your sexual behavior?

HOMEWORK

The purpose of this curriculum is not to change your mind or make you believe in any specific way. Instead, my hope is that this curriculum gives you the opportunity to expand your knowledge and viewpoints to make room for authentically integrating and taking ownership of what you believe to be true about sex and sexuality. The goal is to help you give yourself permission to suspend what you've been taught while you navigate new possibilities.

I'd like you to find a stone that can represent the negative experiences and/or beliefs that are holding back your joy or pleasure. Put the stone to your lips and blow all of the feelings about all the times that joy, desire, or pleasure have died for you. Think about your fears of opening up to receiving the pleasure you deserve in your life and blow that fear into the stone as well. This stone now holds all of these feelings, fears, and experiences. I'd like you to carry around this stone with you everywhere you go until you are ready to let go of the stone and all that it represents. Notice what it feels like to carry the stone with you. Is it annoying? Is it a responsibility? Is it heavy? Once you are ready to release the stone, go to a body of water and throw or place the stone in the water with the intention of healing. (Mindfulness exercise adapted from Ogden, 2008.)

12

✛

Class 5

Desire and Pleasure

OBJECTIVES

- Participants will practice a mindfulness exercise that encourages them to be present (in order to be open to feelings of desire).
- Participants will identify barriers to feelings of desire in their own lives.
- Participants will examine purity culture's effects on desire in their life.
- Participants will evaluate the effects of desire on sexual pleasure.
- Participants will examine the dual control model.

GREETING AND WELCOME

Today we are going to focus on desire. Desire has many names: attraction, passion, love, energy, libido, lust, etc. Gina Ogden (2008) argues that desire "involves the loves, wishes, dreams, memories, fantasies, and meanings that are ongoing parts of our lives" (p. 3). To begin, I would like everyone to find a comfortable place to sit. We are going to use a mindfulness exercise to explore our desire(s) today.

What is mindfulness and how can it help us embrace desire? Mindfulness is the practice of noticing what is happening inside you and of being kind to yourself, even when it's difficult. Mindfulness is giving yourself permission to pay attention—in a neutral, nonjudgmental way (Brotto, 2018). Today we will be using mindfulness to focus on your body, your beliefs about sex, and your emotions related to sex. Mindfulness is the ability to fully inhabit the present moment without trying to change it. It involves accepting who you are and what you are experiencing without judgment (Brotto, 2018). In the foreword to Brotto's book, Emily Nagoski remarks, "Mindfulness improves non-judgmental attention, and non-judgmental attention improves sexual well-being" (p. xi).

How can mindfulness help when it comes to desire? It can help people get in touch with and focus on sensations that are actually happening instead of focusing on imagined or expected outcomes. Women who practice mindfulness see a 60 percent increase in sexual satisfaction, and it teaches women to become more aware of their bodily sensations and sexual sensations. This in turn can improve motivation to pursue sex, notice sexual arousal, and trigger sexual desire (Brotto, 2018).

THE RAISIN

(LORI A. BROTTO)

The mindfulness exercise we are going to begin with today was created by Lori A. Brotto and can be found in her book, *Better Sex Through Mindfulness: How Women Can Cultivate Desire* (2018). I am going to give you each a raisin. As you look at your raisin, I want you to do the following steps:

1. Observe the raisin as if it is the first time you have ever seen a raisin.
2. Notice its shape, size, color, and contour.
3. Notice how the light reflects off its surface.
4. Smell the raisin, taking note of the aromas.
5. Notice how your body responds to the aromas.
6. Lift the raisin to your ear.
7. Notice if the raisin has a sound.
8. Put the raisin against your lips while they are closed.
9. Notice how the raisin feels against your lips.
10. Notice if your mouth or body starts to react to the raisin.
11. Now put the raisin in your mouth and roll it around with your tongue. Do not bite the raisin. What sensations do you notice?
12. Now put the raisin between your teeth and slowly take a bite. Notice what happens, what it feels like and what it tastes like. Are there different flavors?
13. Slowly chew the raisin, noticing how it moves around your mouth and down your throat. Notice the aftertaste.

What did you notice and what sensations did you experience during this exercise? How is this way of paying attention different from how you normally experience the day-to-day events of your life? Is this how you normally eat a raisin? How is eating the raisin like this relevant to desire? How is this relevant to your own sexuality? How might paying attention to a raisin, as you did, be useful or relevant to your current sexual desire? (Brotto, 2018, pp. 74–80).

DESIRE

Female sexual dysfunction affects 15–31 percent of women. Low desire/loss of libido is the most common of these sexual complaints, affecting up to half of women at one point or another in their life. According to the National Survey of Sexual Attitudes and Lifestyles (NATSAL) in Britain, lack of interest in sex is the most common sexual difficulty, affecting one-third of women (Ogden, 2008). The underlying causes of sexual dysfunctions that disrupt desire can be traced to the brain and how the brain processes emotions (Wise, 2019).

To reclaim pleasure, particularly in our sex lives, we need to understand how we are driven by the powerful emotions in our brains (Wise, 2019). A popular myth in our culture is that desire should be spontaneous and randomly show up during everyday life, but for many women, desire takes conscious and intentional preparation (Ogden, 2008). Peggy Kleinplatz and Dana Menard state in their book, *Magnificent Sex: Lessons from Extraordinary Lovers* (2020), that "the notion that sex should be natural and spontaneous ranks among the most difficult assumptions to dislodge" (p. 45). Spontaneous desire just appears, perhaps while casually sitting at lunch or walking down the street, or when you see an attractive person or have a sexual thought. Responsive desire is when you begin to want sex after sexual or erotic things are already happening (Nagoski, 2021). According to Nagoski (2021), "Where spontaneous desire appears in anticipation of pleasure, responsive desire emerges in response to pleasure" (p. 220). While desire may occasionally happen spontaneously, it more often requires prioritization and considerable planning so it can be invited into one's life and/or experience (Nagoski, 2021).

Some researchers believe that desire is not spontaneous but instead is always in response to something (Levine et al., 2016). Nagoski (2021) states that everyone's sexual desire is responsive; it just feels more spontaneous for some people and more responsive for others. In a study of 1,865 women with healthy sexual functioning, one-third stated they never began a sexual experience with a sense of sexual desire; instead, the sexual desire came once the women were aroused (Levine et al., 2016).

Women experience significant shame about their sexual concerns, believing that they should want sex more often, they should enjoy sex more, they should know what they want sexually, they should become aroused quickly, and they should know how to ask for what they want sexually (Brotto, 2018). Do you notice the word "should" popping up a lot? When your inner narrative involves words like "should" or "shouldn't," you are using shaming language.

Oftentimes these shaming narratives were created in us when we were very young by the messages we received from the adults and caregivers in our lives. Whether you have spontaneous or responsive desire, you are normal! Having responsive desire does not mean you have low desire. You can be sexually satisfied while in a healthy relationship and never randomly desire sex (Nagoski, 2021). Research suggests that about half of women may fall into the categories of spontaneous and responsive desire, while the majority of women's desire is context dependent (Nagoski, 2021). In describing desire, Nagoski (2021) suggests, "Desire is pleasure in context" (p. 221).

Ogden, the author of *The Return of Desire* (2008), discusses the four energies of sexual desire. These four energies are physical, emotional, mental, and spiritual. When these four components of sexual desire meet the rigid scripts of what our culture defines sexual desire as they are diametrically opposed. Our understanding of what sexual desire is, as a society, is far too limited. We want to be curious about what sexual desire looks like, feels like, sounds like, and how it affects our sexual experiences. To do this, we have to separate the messages we have been given about sexual desire from what sexual desire truly is so that we can reclaim and redefine our sexual desire.

Our culture has a variety of scripts or narratives about sex. One of these is the romantic script, which states that a boy and a girl fall in love and live happily ever after having amazing sex for the rest of their lives (Ogden, 2008). This script is one of the ones that purity culture adopted, which created unrealistic expectations that left individuals feeling shame or sadness when it didn't play out the way the script promised. When an individual experiences shame, they often internalize the fault, which can create what psychologists refer to as "splitting," which is when someone splits their "good" self from their "bad" self (McClintock, 2001). While this script may be an ideal to strive for, it in no way portrays how sexual emotions come into play. This script insinuates that once you fall in love and get married, everything will work out perfectly when it comes to sex and emotions. Unfortunately, emotions are not always going to be positive, and when difficult emotions arise in these relationships, individuals think there is something wrong or that there is something broken in themselves, which in turn can create fear, guilt, and shame, among other emotions (Ogden, 2008). As Michael Bader (2002) states, "We need to understand the deep level at which shame, rejection, and helplessness extinguish sexual desire" (p. 81). When difficult emotions about desire and sex arise, individuals can become fearful of the emotions, which in turn makes them avoid sex altogether or numb themselves during sexual experiences (Ogden, 2008). According to Ogden (2008), "It's not possible to feel a full longing for pleasure when you've cut yourself off from your most basic emotions and sensations" (p. 8).

Another cultural script is that "good girls" don't like sex and that "good girls" should focus on pleasing their partner(s) when participating in sexual experiences (Ogden, 2008). A "good girl" is polite, modest, a peacekeeper, and submissive. In a world where you are taught to be a "good girl," with the primary message of "good girls don't," how can your sexual desire flourish? How can desire survive when the main goal is to please others? The ability to advocate for and pursue your own pleasure, or to initiate action for your partner's pleasure, and to tell the difference between these two, is fundamental to all relationships. This gives you the ability to express what is real for you, with confidence, responsiveness, and creativity (Martin, 2021). In a sexual relationship where the sole focus is on pleasing your partner, sexual codependency is born (Ogden, 2008). Sexual codependency is the "pattern of focusing on your partner's needs until you lose your sense of self" (Ogden, 2008, p. 65). When in a sexually codependent relationship, we abandon ourselves and our own identity, which in turn eliminates sexual desire (Ogden, 2008).

Another script that women are handed in our culture is the "Oh God" script. This script revolves around the spiritual aspects of sexual desire. It focuses on the belief that if you follow the rules and do everything right, you will experience an amazing connection with your partner and have mind-blowing sex (while on the other hand being expected to have sex when your partner wants to and how they want). Always needing to please your partner(s) while not focusing on your wants, needs, and/or desires creates a feeling of disconnection, which can create disconnection from sexual feelings, numbing, dissociating, and/or creating distractions, which in turn leads to a feeling of loneliness (Ogden, 2008). (This is a good place to stop and allow participants to share what they are feeling and process together.)

According to a feminist psychodynamic developmental perspective, there is significant importance in relationships during female adolescent development when the development of self is connected to relationships and a woman's ability to maintain those close relationships (Impett et al., 2006). During adolescence, girls often fear that if they advocate for themselves, their pleasure, or their knowledge, they will jeopardize their connections with others, and with the world around them (Gilligan, 2003).

One of the ways that women keep these important relationships alive is by silencing their own needs and/or desires to avoid conflict. This is known as "inauthenticity" in relationships (Tolman & Porsche, 2000, p. 365), which is when women hide their true thoughts and feelings. When girls and women silence their needs and desires, they may also struggle to express their sexual needs and/or desires, which is disregarding the self. In a culture that defines sex according to men's desires and denies women's desires, these women may find it extremely difficult to prioritize and/or vocalize their sexual needs (Impett et al., 2006). A woman who is disconnected from her own feelings and emotions may find it difficult to assert or understand her own desires and instead focus on her partner's wants and interests (Tolman, 2002). In a study on sexual health and femininity ideology conducted with high school senior girls, it was found that inauthenticity in relationships and body objectification were both associated with poor sexual self-efficacy. This means that girls who internalized the message that they should "be seen" and "not heard" had less ability to act on their own desires in sexual relationships (Impett et al., 2006). Men are more attentive to their own needs than women are (Fredrickson & Roberts, 1997), and research shows that men's socialization is more self-focused (Prentice & Carranza, 2002) while women are socialized to be more in tune with the needs of others instead of expressing their own desires (Helgeson & Fritz, 1999). Christian resources about sex and marriage often reinforced the idea that men inherently know how to have sex while women do not (Gregoire et al., 2021). It has been found that gender differences can be minimized when women believe they won't be stigmatized for their behavior (Conley et al., 2011). Some Christian organizations believe that pursuing any sort of desire outside of God is sinful. Instead, they focus on fasting, vows of poverty, and celibacy in the hopes that this will shrink the self in order to make more room for the Holy Spirit. They deny themselves desire and pleasure, which can result in hatred and distrust of their bodies (McCleneghan, 2011).

PLEASURE

Humans require the experience of pleasure in life just as much as they need to limit the amount of pain and suffering experienced in their bodies and souls (McCleneghan, 2011). Desire and pleasure often go hand in hand when we talk about sex. Now that you have a basic understanding of what desire is and is not, let's dive into pleasure. The brain is the command center for pleasure (Wise, 2019). Nagoski (2015a) defines pleasure as "a process, not a state, an interaction, not a specific area of the brain or the body. Pleasure is the whole flock. Pleasure is all of you" (p. 287).

Pleasure is "whatever brings you joy and nourishment. Pleasure is a biological guide to what is good for us: fresh air, clean water, food, rest, movement, touch, play" (Martin, 2021, p. 40).

Pleasure is a physiological process that consists of changes in brain activity, blood chemistry, and muscle engagement. You experience pleasure internally. Pleasure can take place in a relaxed state (when the parasympathetic nervous system is engaged) or in an excited state (when your sympathetic nervous system is engaged). The relaxed state is the foundation for pleasure, which we will call your baseline. It is from this baseline that you can go out to play, be curious, and explore. A healthy baseline needs to be a place where you feel safe and that you can learn to access on your own relatively quickly (Martin, 2021). Martin (2021) states that pleasure is "good for you, valuable in its own right, you cannot make it happen, you can learn to access it, you can't give or receive it, you can follow your pleasure, you can't predict where it will take you, you have a pleasure ceiling, it's OK to have mixed feelings about it, and pleasure is a powerful change agent" (pp. 43–44).

Pleasure is a change in your physiology, so if you change your physiology, then you can change what you perceive. When you change what you perceive, then you can change what you can imagine, and if you change what you can imagine, then you can ultimately change your life (Martin, 2021). Wise (2019) remarks, "The experience of pleasure can be described as sexual and sensual, intellectual and fanciful, physical and emotional. It is naturally subjective and can change over time" (p. 15). The feeling of pleasure is internal; it can be a physical sensation and/ or a mental or emotional construct. We can use our brains and bodies to discover, cultivate, and embrace different forms of pleasure (Wise, 2019). Purity culture involved very little information and/or instruction about pleasure. When pleasure was discussed, the focus was on reminding married heterosexual couples who were struggling with pleasure that the focus should be on obedience to God, or to remind wives that they owed their husbands pleasure, regardless of how they personally felt about sex (Emily Allison, 2021).

Many religions taught that sex was solely for procreation and disapproved of behaviors that focused on pleasure (Ashdown et al., 2011). However, we are all born entitled to pleasure. Pleasure has been associated with sin, overindulgence, and the notion that the body is evil. Abstaining from sex has traditionally been seen as virtuous, and the binary idea of body versus soul became the supporting structure for philosophical, religious, artistic, and even scientific thought (Wise, 2019). However, the truth of the matter is that pleasure is entirely subjective— you will have your own sense of what is pleasurable, how many pleasure-inducing activities you desire, how your body experiences pleasure, etc.

Wise (2019) states that pleasure is essential to our emotional, physical, and mental well-being. We often find conflict with pleasure when it comes to sex because we misunderstand our urges, needs, and desires. We are a culture that judges our sexual longings and thus we limit our desires. We do this because at our core we are unhappy, and we need to work hard to redefine our relationship to sex and pleasure (Wise, 2019). Being willing to take charge of your own sexual pleasure will give you the freedom to be the lover you long to be for yourself with or without a partner. While doing so, you may have to face the fear of breaking the rules that may have been portrayed as truths while growing up, rules like needing to depend on a man to fulfill your sexual needs (Ogden, 2008). It's important to remember that too much focus on others undermines healthy self-care, which is essential for good sex and pleasure (Wise, 2019).

Pleasure is a gateway to retrieving your truest self. Pleasure is where you find a carefree connection with yourself and with those you love. Pleasure can only happen in a context where your brain feels safe enough to be your authentic self, without shame or focus on social expectations. When we surrender to pleasure, we are able to experience ecstasy. Remember, you are entitled to and are allowed to like pleasure (Nagoski, 2021). Despite what evangelical messages you may have been given about pleasure, it is important to remember that you do not need to fear knowing or loving your body. Your body is a gift, made to experience pleasure, made for connection to your world and the people in it (McCleneghan, 2011).

Now that we've identified and discussed your right to pleasure, let's focus on how to attain pleasure for yourself. One of the best explanations of what drives pleasure is the dual control model. The dual control model of sexual response was created in the late 1990s by Erik Janssen and John Bancroft at the Kinsey Institute. The dual control model consists of two parts: the sexual excitation system (SE) and the sexual inhibition system (SI). The SE is the accelerator of your sexual response like a gas pedal in a car. It is constantly scanning your environment for sexually relevant stimuli. When it finds that stimuli, it sends the signal from your brain to your genitals to "turn on." The SI is the "off" signal or your sexual brakes (Kinsey Institute, n.d.).

Now that you understand the two parts of the dual control model of sexual response, let's talk about how they work. Basically, your level of sexual arousal is the product of how much stimulation your accelerator is getting and how little stimulation your brakes are getting. What also comes into play is how sensitive your brakes and accelerator are to stimulation. Everyone has a brake and an accelerator, but each individual has different sensitivity of brakes and accelerators. Sensitive brakes, regardless of how the accelerator works, are the strongest predictor of sexual problems (Nagoski, 2021). Men tend to have more sensitive accelerators while women tend to have more sensitive inhibitors, although there are always exceptions. We are all born with accelerator and brake traits that tend to stay the same throughout our lives. While you cannot change the accelerator and brakes, you can often change what they respond to and what your accelerator interprets as sex related. Our culture and environment teach us what stimuli to interpret as excitation or inhibition.

We are all able to mold our context to maximize our sexual potential (Nagoski, 2021). What is context? Context is "how your external circumstances and your internal brain state can influence your sexual responsiveness" (Nagoski, 2021, p. 73). The research shows that women's sexual response tends to be more sensitive to context than men's and that women vary more from one another in how much these factors influence their sexual response (Graham et al., 2006). Growing up in purity culture you may have been encouraged to create and/or focus on contexts that were not sexual and to avoid everything that made you feel aroused or piqued your sexuality. The fear around arousal and sexual stimuli was rampant. Women were often raised in a culture that punished them for embracing and celebrating their bodies. They were taught to fear sex and to be disgusted by all things sex related. This leaves women insecure and anxious, which inevitably slams on their brakes (Nagoski, 2015a). My hope is that you can learn to identify the contexts that make you view the world as an erotic and pleasurable place so that you can ultimately experience sexual satisfaction.

Today I want to leave you with a quote from Emily Nagoski, author of *Come as You Are* (2015a). Nagoski writes,

> The day you were born, the world had a choice about what to teach you about your body. It could have taught you to live with confidence and joy inside your body. It could have taught you that your body and your sexuality are beautiful gifts. But instead, the world taught you to feel critical of and dissatisfied with your sexuality and your body. You were taught to value and expect something from your sexuality that does not match what your sexuality actually is. You were told a story about what would happen in your sexual life, and that story was false. You were lied to. I am pissed, on your behalf, at the world for that lie. And I'm working to create a world that doesn't lie to women about their bodies anymore. (p. 327)

DISCUSSION QUESTIONS

- How did you feel during the mindfulness exercise? Is this an activity (or something similar to it) that you could envision using in your own life?

- What are some barriers to desire in your own life?
- What messages from purity culture do you think have affected the desire in your life?
- What connections do you see between desire and sexual pleasure?
- Can you identify with one side or the other of the dual control model?

HOMEWORK

For homework, I'd like you to go home and take a bath or a shower. As you do so, notice each part of your body. Focus your attention on your body and let your thoughts simply be whatever they need to be. Use all of your senses as you do this. For example, notice the texture of your skin, its color, and what sounds or smells you notice in the bath or shower. Once you have finished and have dried off, spend a few minutes looking at yourself in the mirror. What do you appreciate or like about your body? Are there any body parts that give you a sense of pride or joy? Are there parts of your body that you do not like or appreciate? Your body is alive! What does it feel like? Are there parts of your body that need more attention? Notice any emotions that may come up, both positive and negative. I want you to leave this exercise with the feeling that you fully experienced your body. Throughout the rest of your day, be aware of your body as you move through your routine.

13

✝

Class 6
Masturbation and Self-Exploration

OBJECTIVES

- Participants will define and identify parts of female sexual anatomy.
- Participants will identify and deconstruct messages of shame they received regarding female anatomy and its function/purpose.
- Participants will construct a framework of understanding for the process by which women become aroused (and the physical changes that occur).
- Participants will examine various methods of masturbation.
- Participants will identify and deconstruct messages regarding masturbation.

GREETING AND WELCOME

Welcome back! The focus of today's class may trigger a variety of emotions and/or emotional responses. Please rest assured that I will work to guide the conversation in a light and informative format that leaves the door open for your own exploration. Today, we'll specifically be discussing female sexual anatomy: what it is, how it works, and the messages we have received about our sexual anatomy. Before we begin, let's take a moment to reflect on the messages we have received in the past. I would like everyone to take a marker from the box in the middle of the room and a blank piece of paper. Please take a few minutes to write down all of the words, images, phrases, and messages you have been given/told about female genitalia and the female body. Now, I want you to look at the list in front of you and I want you to circle everything that is positive or up-lifting. I am wondering if you have more circled or uncircled. What are some of the uncircled words, phrases, and/or messages you have on your paper? Now please consider sharing the words, phrases, and/or messages that you have circled. As you can see, our culture has a significant amount of negative and ambivalent attitudes toward female genitalia and female bodies. Why do you think this is? In a culture that celebrates male genitalia and in many ways worships it in pop culture, art, architecture, and more, why is it that we as women feel so much shame about the ways our bodies look, smell, taste, etc.?

INTRODUCTION TO FEMALE GENITALIA

The Vulva

(Hold up a picture of a vulva.) This is a vulva. Take notice that I called it a vulva instead of a vagina. While many of us were taught to call this a vagina, the correct terminology is vulva. What feelings or thoughts come up for you when you look at this picture? Leonore Tiefer (1996) states that ambiguity around female genitalia creates self-doubt in women. Knowing the difference between what the vulva and vagina are and what their functions are is imperative for women. When women do not have a clear understanding of their body parts, it affects their ability to understand their bodies, which can create shame. Harriet Lerner (2004) states that the word "vulva" is intimidating because it is what allows women to experience sexual enjoyment and pleasure, independent from sexual intercourse. She states that our culture avoids using the correct terms for female genitalia because "what is not named does not exist" (p. 166). The clitoris is another part of the vulva that is rarely labeled or dis-cussed. Ogletree and Ginsburg (2000) refer to the lack of addressing the clitoris as a "symbolic clitoridectomy" (p. 924). The silence around the clitoris reinforces society's lack of interest regarding women's sexuality and focuses on vaginal instead of clitoral understandings of women's pleasure, which can negatively affect women's attitudes about their own bodies (Braun & Kitzinger, 2001; Braun & Wilkinson, 2001; Cornog, 1986; Fahs & Frank, 2014; Gartrell & Mosbacher, 1984; Lerner, 1977). The feelings of shame around female genitals are not a new concept. Believe it or not, in Renaissance times, the vulva was often referred to as "pudendum," which is Latin for "to be ashamed" (Mintz, 2017, p. 38). Female sexuality has been judged and shamed throughout history, often because it was not understood and was viewed as a threat by men. Be-fore we get into deeper discussions on the vulva, let us review the basic

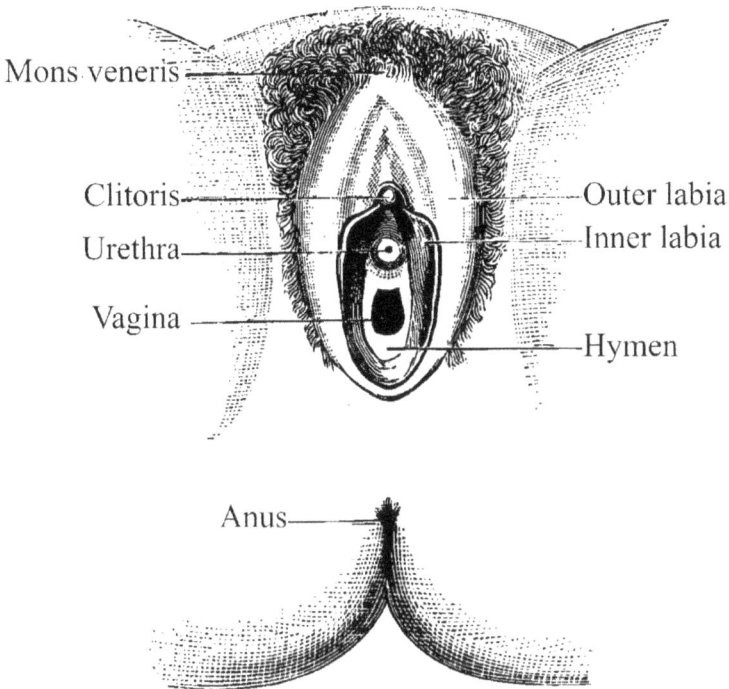

Figure 13.1 Vulva anatomy. From *Handbook of Obstetric Nursing*, 2nd ed., by Francis W. N. Haultain & James Haig Ferguson, 1894, J. B. Lippincott Company, via Wikipedia (https://commons.wikimedia.org/wiki/File:Haultain_and_Ferguson_-_external_female _genital_organs.svg).

terminologies to ensure we are all starting on the same page. (Refer to picture of the vulva.) These are the outer lips of the vulva; their job is to surround and protect the more delicate parts inside. The outer lips come in many different sizes and thicknesses, which is completely normal. Interestingly, modern pornography has had a tremendous impact on creating the perception that there is only one "normal" standard for outer lips. In truth, the size, shape, and thickness of these lips vary tremendously from vulva to vulva. This is the urethral opening that connects to the urethra, a short tube that connects to the bladder. This opening is where urine exits the body. This is the vaginal opening, which is the opening to the canal inside your body known as the vagina. The vaginal canal is a collection of tissue, highly sensitive nerves, and blood vessels. When a woman is aroused, the vagina will actually self-lubricate (get wet) and change size and shape in preparation for penetration. When aroused, the vagina goes through a process known as vaginal tenting. The vagina narrows in the front and gets wider in the back, in addition to elongating. The vagina expands from 3–4 inches to 5–6 inches long, enabling it to accommodate a finger, insertable toy, object, or penis. The vaginal opening and the first third of the vaginal canal have a lot of sensitive nerve endings, while the inner two-thirds of the vaginal canal has almost no touch-sensitive nerve endings. Interestingly, the back of the vaginal canal is more sensitive to pressure than to touch. This makes vaginal childbirth less painful (believe it or not) because when the baby is lodged in the vaginal canal, there is less pain in the vaginal canal due to a lack of sensitive nerve endings. The mons pubis is a mound of fatty tissue that is on top of the pubic bone and is filled with nerve endings. The mons pubis is also what covers and protects the clitoris. The clitoral hood is a loose collection of skin that covers the clitoral glans. In some women, the hood completely covers the glans, while in others it only partially covers it. Like the outer lips, clitoral hoods come in many shapes, sizes, and colors. The inner lips of the vulva are filled with erectile tissue and when aroused become engorged with blood, causing them to double or even triple in size. The inner lips are usually asymmetrical and change color when a woman is aroused (Mintz, 2017). On either side of the entrance to the vagina, there are two glands called the Bartholin glands. These glands release fluid during sexual arousal to help reduce friction during penetration and/or create a scent that communicates health and fertility (Nagoski, 2015a).

The Clitoris

The clitoris is a smooth, round bump that is covered in 6,000–8,000 nerve endings and has no known bodily function except to create pleasure (Mintz, 2017). Based on this, it seems that the female body is inherently designed to not only have sex but to enjoy it. The clitoris is made of erectile tissue that swells when it gets stimulated. When a woman is aroused and stimulated, the blood flow in the vagina increases and the blood flow to the clitoris increases to 4–11 times the baseline (Chadwick, 2021). When viewed externally, you can only see a small part of the clitoris from the outside of the vulva. The remainder of the clitoris extends internally, including two long arms that are about 3.5 inches long, accompanied by a pair of fleshy bulbs that reach about 2.75 inches long (Chadwick, 2021). Here is a picture of the entire clitoris (show picture of clitoris). Chadwick (2021) states, "for women, the clitoris is uniquely central to an orgasmic experience" (p. 160). The clitoris is an imperative part of the female sexual experience because for many women it doesn't matter how much clitoral stimulation they get from vaginal penetration; it will not result in an orgasm, while direct stimulation to the clitoral glans will almost always result in an orgasm (Chadwick, 2021).

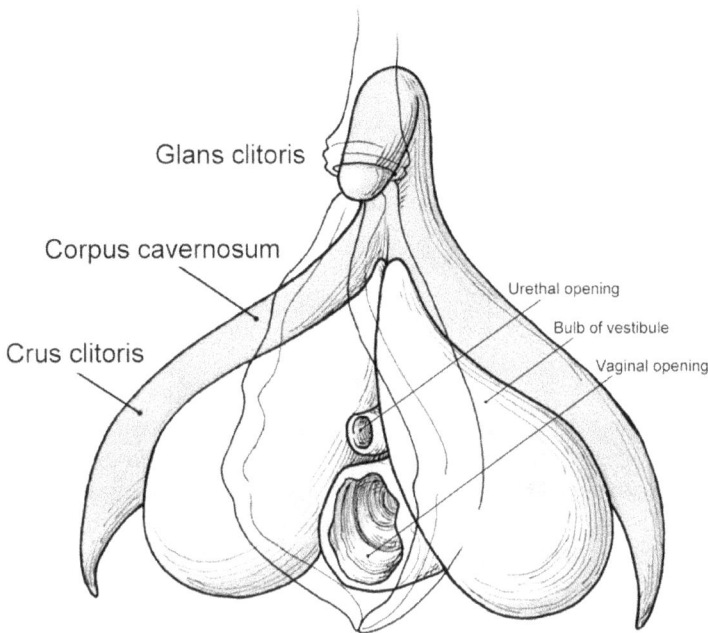

Figure 13.2 Clitoris anatomy. Illustration by Amphis [user], 2007, Wikipedia (https://commons.wikimedia.org/wiki/File:Clitoris_anatomy_labeled-en.jpg).

ORGASM

Now that we know the parts of female sexual anatomy and how each part of the vulva and vagina works, we want to talk about orgasms. What is an orgasm? Put simply, an orgasm is "the sudden, involuntary release of sexual tension" (Nagoski, 2015a, p. 267). To be honest, every orgasm is different and there isn't a gold standard of orgasm. There isn't a right kind or better kind of orgasm. Despite what you may have read in magazines and/or seen in the media there is no clitoral vs. anal vs. vaginal orgasm. Every orgasm is a sudden release of sexual tension, generated in different ways. Some women feel a rhythmic pulsing of the muscle around their vagina and then other times they don't. Orgasms can change in length, intensity, and feeling depending on where you are in your menstrual cycle, depending on the type of stimulation, whether you have reached menopause, or whether you are with a partner or by yourself. Most women state that they feel a sense of completion or "doneness"; a peak of tension where their muscles tighten followed by a pleasurable release (Nagoski, 2015a). Emily Nagoski (2015a) states that orgasms are "like art. . . . You know when you see it" or in most cases, feel it. She continues, "Orgasm is not a genital response, 'pleasure,' hierarchical, or an evolutionary adaptation" (p. 267). It's not uncommon to have never experienced an orgasm or to not be sure if you have experienced an orgasm. The expression of orgasm can also vary widely (despite what our media tells us). If any of you have seen the movie *When Harry Met Sally*, you have watched the scene where Sally pretends to have an orgasm while out to eat with Harry. It's completely acceptable and healthy to be quiet while having an orgasm or to put your head in a pillow, or to laugh, or scream, or moan. However you experience or express your orgasm is perfect! What matters most is that you are authentically you. Our culture often focuses on reaching orgasm when it comes to sex despite the fact that orgasm makes up 1 percent or less of a sexual experience (Klein, 2012). The remaining 99 percent of a sexual experience is just as important, if not more important, than an orgasm. Focusing on performance (e.g., did I orgasm or not?) versus pleasure can negatively affect an entire sexual experience. Marty Klein (2012) states that in order to keep sex free of performance anxiety, we don't want to take our partner's preferences, limitations, or sexual functioning personally.

MASTURBATION

Now that we know what the vulva looks like and what each part's function is, what can we do with it? This can be an uncomfortable topic for some. That's all right. Keep in mind that we have created a safe and inclusive place to learn more about our bodies. When it comes to the topic of masturbation, it is very important that you learn about your own body and how it works before you expect someone else to understand your body. Masturbation can be a tool that helps you define yourself, your needs, and your desires, which can help you build intimacy with others (McCleneghan, 2011). Growing up with the sex-negative messages from purity culture, we often feel shame or remorse when we masturbate or even consider exploring our own bodies. It is not surprising if you have experienced these feelings. In purity culture, women are often taught that their sexuality should be focused on others and that it is about giving pleasure to their partner(s). Purity culture often shames individuals for seeking knowledge and understanding about their bodies (Anderson, 2015). What are some of the messages you received about masturbation growing up? (Give participants time to share.) Let us focus on what the actual messages were and where they came from. Your family, your church, your peers, and even popular culture probably played a role in the messages you received. These messages have directly impacted the way you view your genitals, self-pleasure, and sexuality.

Up until 1968, masturbation was a diagnosable condition in the *Diagnostic and Statistical Manual of Mental Disorders*, published by the American Psychiatric Association; in 1972 masturbation was defined as "normal" (Chadwick, 2021). We know from research that individuals who grew up in the midst of purity culture were often not encouraged to be curious about their bodies and/or sexual pleasure, which meant they did not develop a sense of sexual play or enjoyment (Sellers, 2017). In 2009, the National Survey of Sexual Health and Behavior from Indiana University, which is the largest nationally representative study of sexual and sexual-health behaviors, surveyed 5,865 Americans between the ages of 14 and 94. They found that approximately 20 percent of women between the ages of 20 and 40 reported that they had never masturbated (Herbenick et al., 2010). In this same study, they found that on average 66 percent of women ages 18 to 39 had masturbated in the past year. While this study did not look at the correlation between lack of masturbation and guilt, Laurie Mintz, the author of *Becoming Cliterate* (2017), surveyed her students about masturbation and found that 11 percent of the women had never masturbated while 89 percent had. Out of that 89 percent, about one-third felt guilty about masturbating. According to Mintz, for many women, guilt is directly correlated to masturbation for a few main reasons: (1) individuals' lack of information about masturbation and/or their bodies, (2) the taboo nature of the topic, and (3) the perception of masturbation as sinful or unhealthy. Many religions have negative views about masturbation. In evangelical Christian circles, masturbation is often referred to as the "secret sin" and is perceived as a threat to the survival of mankind (Patton, 1985). Michael Patton states that masturbation is a means of sexual pleasure but that it has been judged and misunderstood by medical and religious experts. According to Patton (1985), "There has been no other form of sexual activity that has been more frequently discussed, more roundly condemned, and more universally practiced than masturbation" (p. 134).

One might wonder where evangelical Christians got the idea that masturbation is a sin. For many, this belief is tied to the story of Onan in the Book of Genesis. According to Genesis 38:7–10, after the death of Onan's brother, Onan was required by Jewish law to have sex with and impregnate his brother's wife, Tamar, in order to carry on his brother's family line. Onan did indeed have sex with his brother's widow, but he withdrew his penis before ejaculating (also known as "coitus interruptus"), "spilling his seed" outside of her body (Knowles, 2002). As the story goes, this resulted in God striking him dead. It is believed that this is the root of Judeo-Christian attitudes about masturbation, also known as onanism. Onan had sex with Tamar, but he denied her the means to protect or sustain herself by having an heir, which means that Onan pursued his own pleasure at the cost of Tamar, who as a woman was vulnerable to him. This is what was displeasing to God, not the fact that he did not ejaculate inside her. The actual sin was the fact that Onan broke the relationship and commitment to Tamar, which in turn harmed her. The sin was not the pleasure (McCleneghan, 2011). Ironically, Jesus never spoke about masturbation in the Bible. In fact, there is evidence that the belief that masturbation is sinful was developed by the early church (Patton, 1985). Other than this one reference to "spilling his seed," the Bible mentions very little about masturbation (and nothing about female masturbation). The first indications of formal church doctrine regarding masturbation can be traced to an influential bishop in the early Christian church, Augustine. Augustine specifically taught that masturbation and other forms of outercourse were worse than sex outside of marriage, incest, rape, or adultery. Augustine felt that masturbation was sinful because it was a form of contraception, while fornication, incest, rape, or adultery could lead to pregnancy (Knowles, 2002). Even without a biblical doctrine to impart guidance on the topic of masturbation, a study by sociologist J. Kenneth Davidson (1995) found that women who frequently attended religious services were more likely to view masturbation as being unhealthy and sinful. These same women were ashamed to admit they masturbated and felt guilty about masturbating. In 1994, researchers found that about half of men and women who masturbate experienced some kind of guilt (Laumann et al., 1994). Once you realize that many of purity culture's stances on masturbation are the direct result of patriarchal influences (rather than biblical influences), you begin to find the real reason that masturbation was discouraged and looked down on. Masturbation is a way to connect with yourself that brings pleasure (and often orgasm). It is a natural bodily process that deserves neither the shame nor stigma attached to it. Dopamine levels in the brain increase 400 percent during an orgasm (Roberts, 2020). Your body was designed to enjoy orgasms (and the pleasant sensations that come with orgasm). According to a study in 1994, more than 50 percent of women in their thirties masturbate and people who have regular sex partners, live with a partner, and/or are married are more likely to masturbate than people without sexual partners (Michael et al., 1994). Take note that sexual health and medical professionals like Betty Dodson (1996) state that masturbation or "self-loving" has physical, emotional, relationship, and sexual benefits. Purity culture often emphasized the myth that if you waited to have sex until marriage then you would experience unendingly pleasurable and satisfying sex. Unfortunately, individuals who chose to wait until marriage to engage in sexual activity often didn't have this experience. Tina Schermer Sellers, a well-known Christian sex therapist and author of *Sex, God, and the Conservative Church* (2017), discusses this recurring letdown. Sellers states that purity culture typically promises a "happily ever after" for individuals who wait to have sex until marriage, marry another Christian, and choose to raise their children in the church. Unfortunately, many people who believe this promise and follow the rules find that the promise does not come to fruition (Sellers, 2017). One of the missing components in a successful sex life is an awareness of one's own body (and what brings pleasure). Jon Knowles, lead author of the Planned Parenthood white paper "Masturbation: From Stigma to Sexual Health" (2002), notes, "We learn from our own experiences with our bodies and minds what it is we like, what it is we don't like, how and where we like to be touched, what turns us off, and what turns us on." How can someone else know how to touch your body or what makes you feel good when you yourself don't know? Masturbation is a way to explore yourself and figure out what you like and what feels good. When you know your own body, you are then able to teach someone else about your body's needs.

HOW DO YOU MASTURBATE?

This may seem like an obvious answer for some. But I often find women who lived through purity culture have missed out on the experimentation that can result in a deep understanding of their bodies. Therefore, we will start with the basics and work our way up (or down). There is no one right way to masturbate. One could fill an entire book with female masturbation methods and techniques. Some women enjoy digital (finger) penetration while stimulating their clitoris, while others hump pillows or other inanimate objects. Some women use insertable toys or objects to masturbate, while others use pressurized water in the tub. Some women use electric vibrating toothbrushes or even hairbrushes. There is no right or wrong way to masturbate. What matters most is that you take the time to explore your body and to be curious about what brings you pleasure. One key piece of consistency is that 95 percent of women require clitoral stimulation in order to reach orgasm (Mintz, 2017). This statistic stands in contrast to traditional messages about sex (e.g., that penile penetration is the only method capable of bringing a woman to orgasm). Unfortunately, we live in a penis-centered culture where we have been told that a woman needs penetration to orgasm and that if you do not orgasm from penetration alone there is something wrong with you. According to Paula Bennett (1993), the emphasis on vaginal, as opposed to clitoral, sexuality promotes a woman's need for a man to obtain sexual fulfillment. Elisabeth Lloyd's (2005) research suggests that a quarter of women can reliably experience an orgasm through vaginal penetration alone. Despite the fact that the majority of women need clitoral stimulation to experience orgasm, interaction with the clitoris is frequently considered merely the preface to intercourse or what is considered "real sex" (Hungrige, 2016; Pitts & Rahman, 2001; Sanders & Reinisch, 1999). I want to make sure that you hear me loud and clear when I say that this is a complete lie! Mintz (2017) found in her study that 78 percent of women's orgasm problems during sexual encounters including intercourse are caused by a lack of clitoral stimulation or by the wrong kind of clitoral stimulation. Nan Wise states in her book *Why Good Sex Matters* (2019) that "even with additional clitoral stimulation, less than half of women (43 percent) report experiencing orgasm through intercourse 75 percent of the time" (p. 197). The pinnacle of the heterosexual hierarchy is vaginal intercourse, which means that vaginal intercourse is the sexual activity that is "the most 'serious,' the most dangerous, the most enjoyable, the most intimate, the godliest, the most 'natural,' or the most 'normal'" (Klein, 2012, p. 143).

One of the greatest resources I have discovered for women exploring their bodies is a website called OMG Yes. OMG Yes is a website that was created by women for women and it's all about masturbation and female pleasure. If you are ever interested in learning about different masturbation techniques or would like to watch short videos of everyday women talking about and showing you what brings them pleasure, I highly recommend this site.

PORNOGRAPHY

A hot-button issue in evangelical Christianity is the use of pornography. Many evangelical churches teach that the use of pornography is sinful and should be avoided. As sexual gatekeepers, women are taught that it is their responsibility to protect themselves and the men in their community from sexual sin. In many of the Christian books written about marriage, authors insinuate that sex is the way that men handle their sexual temptation. A man who has enough sex is less likely to be tempted. If a man doesn't have his sexual needs met by his wife, then he is more likely to fall into sinful behavior like watching porn. While women are not responsible for their husband's sin, they are told that their husband is more likely to watch porn or engage in sexual sin if his wife does not meet his sexual needs. Women are encouraged to have sex with their husbands to keep them sexually satisfied to help decrease the likelihood of them sinning, watching porn, or looking for sexual gratification outside of the marriage. In a poll of evangelical Christian women conducted by Sheila Wray Gregoire and colleagues (2021), it was found that many women believed that they needed to have sex with their husbands to prevent them from looking at or using pornography. Out of the women who held this belief,

19 percent experienced sexual pain. These same women were 37 percent more likely to have sex out of obligation or fear and 38 percent of these women were unsatisfied with the level of emotional closeness they experienced during sex. The belief that women are responsible to meet the sexual needs of their husbands and that if they fail in this, their husbands will most likely look outside of the marriage creates tremendous pressure on women. Pressure kills pleasure and can create performance anxiety. Women who are engaging in sexual acts out of fear or because they feel that it's their wifely duty are less likely to be present during a sexual act, less likely to experience pleasure, and more than likely not engaging in sexual acts that they desire. This framework reinforces the narrative that women are responsible to give pleasure to men and to keep men from sinning. It sends the message that men are unable to control their sexual urges and/or appetite. Where does self-awareness and self-control come in? There is no need for men to own their behavior if the belief is that women are fully responsible. Evangelicals teach that porn use is sinful and that it draws an individual in and ultimately changes the way they view sex. They state that porn is "not relational, mutual, or loving" (Gregoire et al., 2021, p.118). Instead, they believe that porn is "degrading, violent, and purely carnal" (Gregoire et al., 2021, p. 118). While everyone is entitled to their own opinion on porn and/or masturbation, it is important to ask yourself some deeper questions. What messages did you receive about porn? What are your feelings about porn use? Is porn the actual issue for you or is masturbating to porn the issue?

SEX TOYS AND LUBE

Most women use their hands and/or fingers to masturbate when they first explore masturbation. While this is a completely healthy way to masturbate, it can sometimes take a longer time to reach orgasm. For this reason, many women experiment with objects that they find around the home that create vibration or friction. There is no way I can go over every sex toy on the market, but I thought it might be helpful to talk about some of the different kinds of sex toys on the market to give you a good place to start. In the world of sex toys, many are poorly made and routinely fail to give the experience you desire. When searching for quality masturbation aids, I recommend seeking out premium women-led companies. These companies typically use higher-quality internal components and have worked hard to develop a product that works for vulva owners. Bear in mind, not all toys will work for all people. We're all different. Our bodies come in a variety of shapes and sizes, and we respond in different ways to stimulation. The important part is not to give up when exploring the

world of sex toys. When it comes to masturbating, one of the most popular kinds of sex toys for vulva owners are clitoral stimulators. These are
sex toys that do not typically involve vaginal penetration and primarily
focus on clitoral stimulation. They can blow air or use suction or vibration to stimulate the clitoris. (Show pictures of 3–4 clitoral stimulators.)
For individuals who like vaginal penetration and clitoral stimulation at
the same time, these are a few basic models. (Show pictures of 3–4 toys.)
Some of these stimulate the back of the clitoris by pulsating on what used
to be referred to as the G-spot, which is in fact the back of the clitoris.
Other vibrators that you insert into the vaginal canal have a part that vi-
brates on the clitoris at the same time. (Show 3–4 examples.) Some women
prefer to stimulate their own clitoris while inserting a toy or object at the
same time. Since many women feel that sex toys are too intense when
placed directly on the clitoris, it can be more pleasurable to use their fingers or hand while also experiencing the feeling of penetration with a toy
that does not vibrate. For women who enjoy grinding or humping during
masturbation, there are a number of products on the market that assist in
this form of stimulation.

Using a good lubricant when masturbating with your fingers or toys
can make the experience more pleasurable. While many women create
their own lubrication as they become aroused, it can't hurt to have extra
lubrication to help protect your vulva and vagina during masturbation.
(Show Good Clean Love, Sliquid, and Uber lube.)

For women who struggle with anxiety around sex, vaginal penetration,
or who've experienced vaginal pain during penetration, I recommend
using a lubricant with CBD or THC in it because it can help calm the
vulva and vagina. (Show picture of Foria.) If you've never ordered any of
these products, you may be wondering how they are packaged and sent
to your home. Rest assured that these companies package their products
discreetly and that no one should be able to tell what is in the package.
Some women get worried about searching for sex toys or products online
because they aren't sure what they will come across. Here are some safe
sites to go to; they all offer a variety of payment methods if you want to
avoid the purchases showing on your credit card statement: bellesa bou-
tique, pink cherry, babeland.

Care of toys is extremely important since many of these toys and
products can be on the more expensive side, and you want to get a lot
of use out of them. It is important to clean your toys after each use.
ToyLife foaming toy cleaner is an antibacterial cleaner that works
on all types of toys, or you can always use warm water and soap.
Washing your toys decreases the likelihood of getting vaginal and/or
anal infections. Knowing what types of lubes to use with your toys is
also important. Most high-end sex toys are made of silicone because

silicone is a body-safe material that feels realistic and lasts for a long time, unlike plastic or jelly toys. You do not want to use silicone-based lubricants with silicone toys because they will break down the toys. Instead, you want to use water- or oil-based lubricant with silicone toys. Water-based lubricants are easy to clean up and are gentle and soothing to the skin. Unfortunately, water-based lubricant tends to evaporate quickly and can become sticky. Oil-based lubricant lasts longer, doesn't evaporate quickly, and is hydrating. Bear in mind that oil-based lubricants do break down latex, so you want to be careful when using latex condoms. Silicone-based lubricants are safe to use with toys that are not silicone-based (e.g., plastic, aluminum, ceramic, steel, glass, and marble; Russo, 2021).

DISCUSSION QUESTIONS

- How many of you have looked at your genitalia closely with a mirror?
- Were there any parts of female anatomy you were unaware of?
- Was there something that surprised you about female anatomy?
- What were some of the shameful messages you received in purity culture regarding female genitalia?
- Were there any methods of masturbation or orgasm that intrigued you?
- What were some of the shameful messages you received regarding masturbation?

HOMEWORK

How many of you have ever looked at your vulva? I mean really stopped to admire her and see what she is all about? I want you all to go home tonight and between now and our next class I'd like you to take out a mirror and look at your vulva. Notice the colors and shapes of your vulva. Notice the feelings that come up inside you when you look at your vulva. Be curious about your vulva and find at least one thing that you like about your vulva. It's OK if this feels weird or uncomfortable. It may take a few tries. Your vulva is no different from any other part of your body, although the importance or value that our culture, religion, and families have taught us to assign to them is different. While doing your homework, think about what came up for you. What were your responses or thoughts? Journal what this experience was like for you, what internalized messages you had, and what feelings came up.

14

✢

Class 7

Conclusion

OBJECTIVES

- Participants will reflect on the effects of the purity culture on their sexual experiences.
- Participants will deconstruct the sexual messages they received in purity culture in order to develop new sexual ethics and viewpoints.
- Participants will experience a guided meditation (in order to promote its use in the future by the participant).

(This final class was written from the perspective of the author and would need to be changed based on the person leading the class. The author encourages anyone who uses this curriculum to be creative in this final class and to make it your own. Everything written is simply an example.)

GREETING AND WELCOME

I want to start our class off today with a quote from Steve Allen: "History, of course, is tragically full of examples where well-intentioned spiritual convictions led directly to suppression of contrary views, oppression, torture, war, and other atrocities, all in the name of what was supposedly holy" (as cited in Winell, 1993, p. vii). While creating these classes, this is the quotation I kept circling back to that helped me stay focused and centered. I wrote my book and these classes because I wanted to give women who received the messages of and participated in the indoctrination of purity culture a different perspective on pleasure, sex, and sexuality. My goal was not and will never be to change someone's beliefs or religion. My goal is not to change what anyone believes or tell them how to live their life. Instead, my goal is to take my life experiences, my education, and what I've learned as a doctor of clinical sexology and a certified sex therapist and present evidence-based information to give women the freedom to decide for themselves what they desire and ultimately what they believe is right for them. My hope is that this seven-week class has given you the space to be curious and open—the space to feel safe, heard, and seen—the space to express your feelings, desires, fears, and everything in between. Purity culture gave you a set of values around sex and sexuality and you were told that because these were community values, they had to be your values. You were not given a choice about adopting these values (Smith, 2020). Despite what the messages of purity culture told you, we do not live in a world that is black and white. We live in a world of gray consisting of many religions, ideas, cultures, lifestyles, and experiences. It is my hope that what you learned in these classes and the ensuing reflections has enabled you to define your own values so you can be more confident in making decisions around sex, pleasure, and your sexuality. It is my firm belief that if there is a god or a higher power, they would want us to ask questions, lean into vulnerability, and ultimately grow into the beautiful people we are capable of being. Pleasure is your birthright! Purity culture taught you to reject and neglect your body, to separate from it and live in your mind. I want you to know that "your physical body is you as much as your mental, emotional, and spiritual dimensions" (Winell, 1993, p. 225). Your body is not simply a vessel or "flesh"; it is your closest friend, it is what allows you to experience this world, it is beautiful and truly amazing! Your body and your sexuality are exquisite and belong solely to you.

GARDEN EXERCISE

(Hand out the garden projects from the first session.) Look at the garden in front of you. (Give them five minutes to look at the gardens.) How does this garden make you feel as you look at it? Do you see any weeds or plants you'd like to pull out now? Are there any new flowers or plants that you would like to add to your garden? Would you label the places in your garden the same way? (Hand out blank pieces of paper.) I am now giving each of you a new piece of paper for you to design and create a new garden when you go home. As you make your new garden, I want you to think back over the past seven weeks—think about what you've learned and how you've changed. As you create your new garden, you will be the only person who knows what has changed, what has been removed, and what has been added. What is most important is that you are the master gardener of your garden, and you get to choose what seeds, flowers, plants, and weeds will be in this garden.

WHAT COMES NEXT?

As we look back over the past seven weeks of learning together, what are some of the most helpful things you learned? Are there questions you still have? I'd love for everyone who feels comfortable sharing, to share a word, thought, question, or feeling that they've learned about or felt was helpful during this class. If you're still unsure of where you are and are still in the process of putting together the pieces, that's OK. For some of you, this is the end of your exploration into purity culture, and I want to thank you for being willing to step out of your daily life and your comfort zone to learn. For others, this may be the very beginning of a whole new chapter of self-discovery, and I want to encourage you to keep an open mind as you continue in this journey. Some of you may be experiencing grief about what you might feel you have lost. You may feel you have lost a sense of identity, faith, sexuality, core beliefs, etc. Grief can show itself in different ways like denial, anger, sadness, isolation, or confusion. There is no "right" way to experience grief. What is most important is that you give yourself the time and space you need to acknowledge and process your grief in order to heal and move forward. Over the past seven weeks, all of you have attended either individual or couples therapy outside of the group in the hopes that it would give you the support you needed as you processed difficult feelings and beliefs that may have come up in the group. Grief is something that often arises during the deconstruction process, so if you are experiencing grief, please know that you are not alone. I encourage you to continue working with a mental health professional to help you process this grief as you continue on your journey. If you would like to find a therapist who specializes in grief, you can find local therapists at https://www.psychologytoday.com/us. For anyone who feels they would like to continue looking into their history with purity culture and the effects it has had and continues to have on their life, I would recommend finding a therapist who is well-versed in religious trauma and/or sex therapy. For a list of certified sex therapists, you can go to the American Association of Sexuality Educators, Counselors and Therapists website at https://www.aasect.org. For therapists who understand religious trauma and/or religious culture, you can go to https://www.journeyfree.org. Some of the most helpful books I have found that address the topic of purity culture are:

1. *Pure* by Linda Kay Klein;
2. *You Are Your Own* by Jamie Lee Finch;
3. *#Churchtoo* by Emily Joy Allison;
4. *Damaged Goods* by Dianna E. Anderson;
5. *Sex, God, and the Conservative Church* by Tina Schermer Sellers;
6. *Beyond Shame* by Matthias Roberts;
7. *Sexual Shame* by Karen A. McClintock;
8. *Jesus and John Wayne* by Kristin Kobes Du Mez;
9. *The Making of Biblical Womanhood* by Beth Allison Barr; and
10. *Good Christian Sex* by Bromleigh McCleneghan.

For books on understanding your bodies and sexuality, I recommend:

1. *Come as You Are* by Emily Nagoski;
2. *Becoming Cliterate* by Laurie Mintz;
3. *Why Good Sex Matters* by Nan Wise;
4. *Better Sex Through Mindfulness* by Lori A. Brotto; and
5. *Sexual Intelligence* by Marty Klein.

I would like to close our time together with a guided meditation to help calm and center you into your body and your pleasure. Please close your eyes and get as comfortable as you can. Begin to focus on your breath as you breathe in and out, filling your belly with the inhale and fully emptying it with the exhale. Notice if there are any places in your body that feel tight or tense or sore. Intentionally breathe into those places, giving them permission to let go and relax. Now draw your attention to your heart—and to your mind. Notice if there are any feelings, fears, or beliefs that you wish to release, and if so, imagine releasing them from your body with the next exhale. Remember that your breath is what connects you to your body, mind, heart, and spirit. As you continue to breathe, imagine the breath moving around and through your entire being. Now that you feel calm and connected to your emotional and physical self, I want you to imagine a time or a place when you felt pleasure. It could be the sound of a loved one's voice or the waves crashing on the sand. Perhaps it's the feeling of moss under your feet or the warmth of a soft blanket surrounding your body. Allow yourself to go to a memory where you felt immersed in pleasure and remember how good you felt. Notice where you felt that pleasure in your body and what the pleasure felt like. Perhaps it had a sound, or a color associated with it. Allow yourself to completely sink into that pleasure. Now imagine that pleasure giving you power—the kind of power that you would want to share with someone else. As you continue to breathe in and out, imagine that power filling your body, mind, heart, and spirit. Picture yourself filled with and surrounded by pleasure and power. Where are you? Are you alone? What is your body doing? What is all around you? Be curious about what is happening to and around you. Allow yourself to fully melt into this place of pleasure and power. Now imagine that pleasure and power filling your feet—up into your legs—and your thighs—into your pelvis and your buttocks—around to your back and up into your neck and shoulders—down through your arms and into your hands—then back up through your arms into your neck and your head. Imagine the breath leaving through the top of your head and turning into light. The light then enters back into your body, filling your head, neck, shoulders, arms, hands, back, pelvis, buttocks, legs, and out through the bottom of your feet. As you look at your body that is filled with pleasure, power, and light, you suddenly notice a being walking toward you. Perhaps it is an old friend, or a pet, or someone you don't even know. As this being approaches you, they hand you a piece of paper that has your name on it. This is a message for you—a message about pleasure. Emotional, physical, intellectual, and sexual pleasure. This message reminds you that you are deserving of pleasure—all pleasure. It is your birthright, and is what you need more of in your life. As you soak in this message and all that it means for you, allow yourself to send that message to your heart. Breathe in all that is pleasurable for you—give yourself permission to pursue every kind of pleasure that you desire. Know that you can access this kind of connection, power, and pleasure any time that you like through the simple act of breathing it into yourself. Know that you are strong—that you are beautiful—that you are deserving of pleasure. And whenever you are ready you can open your eyes and come back into the room.

Thank you for being willing to be vulnerable with me during that mindfulness activity. It is my hope that it helped you connect to yourself in a new way after everything we have worked through together on this journey. Make note of anything that came to mind during that guided meditation. Perhaps you want to look at it or journal about it later when you go home. Notice how it felt to focus on your body and pleasure. I know that for many of you this is the beginning of your healing journey. It is my hope that the topics we have discussed and the things we have learned during our time together have awakened curiosity in you. The journey of self-discovery and healing is never completely over, and it is my hope that you continue to ask questions and grow so you can become the best version of you. It has been a privilege to work with all of you over the past seven weeks, and I wish you well as you continue in your individual journeys.

15

✛

Epilogue

Evangelical Christian purity culture has affected generations of men, women, and couples. It has impacted their ability to experience pleasure, has given them unrealistic expectations about sex, and instilled sexual guilt and shame. Within the past ten to fifteen years, the stories and lived experiences of individuals affected by these teachings and beliefs have begun to emerge. In memoirs, on podcasts, and in the therapy room, people are talking about their lived experiences and how the sex-negative messaging has affected or is impacting their lives. In the world of sex therapy, we are seeing more and more clients who struggle with lack of sexual desire and sexual dysfunction due to the teachings around abstinence and purity. Many of these individuals struggle with disconnection from their bodies, pleasure, and sexuality. There is a tremendous need for therapists and mental health professionals who understand the teachings and beliefs of evangelical Christian purity culture. Professionals who understand this culture are more likely able to meet individuals from this population in a way that they feel seen, heard, and supported on their journey of healing. As someone who was indoctrinated by the teachings of purity culture, I have always longed for my experiences to be acknowledged and believed. My feelings and experiences were often silenced by the religion and the evangelical community with whom I grew up. I decided to write this book because it was a way for me to share my story, but to also validate the experiences of women who were exposed to the teachings of purity culture. It is my hope that this book has brought some clarity to what purity culture is and how it has affected women. We all deserve to share our story and to have our experiences validated. While not everyone who lived through purity culture had a negative experience, many of us did. This book is for those of us who struggle in our personal and sexual lives. It is for the partners of people who carry the pain in their bodies and minds. Many of us have spent most of our lives believing there was something wrong with us or that we were broken. No matter what you believe or who you are, it is my hope that you see that you have the ability to change the narrative and in turn change the way you view yourself, pleasure, and sex. There is a significant need for more research on the effects of purity culture on men, women, members of the LGBTQIA+ community, and relationships. As you end this book, I want you to know that you are entitled to experience and embrace pleasure—emotional, intellectual, physical, and sexual pleasure. Pleasure is your birthright.

Appendix
Informed Consent Form

(Insert location and address of where class will be held)

**WELCOME TO YOUR GROUP
CURRICULUM/WORKSHOP EXPERIENCE!**

Please read the following information thoroughly. The intent of this document is to better inform you about participating in a psychoeducational group and outline the expectations and responsibilities of both the members and the facilitating therapist. You are welcome to discuss questions/concerns regarding this document with your facilitating therapist at any time. If you decide to participate in the Deconstructing Purity Culture to Embrace Sexual Pleasure class, please fill in and sign the bottom of this form so that we will have a record that you have read the information and are properly informed about the details pertaining to this type of psychoeducational workshop experience. All participants are required to attend individual or couples therapy with a licensed mental health professional in conjunction with attending this psychoeducational group. This requirement has been made to facilitate your processing any emotional conflicts or difficulties that could arise (given the nature of the curriculum's subject matter). Deconstruction or challenging one's core beliefs can impact an individual's entire family system, which is why outside professional support is required. Due to the sensitive topic of this curriculum and the time constraints of the individual classes, there will not be sufficient time or resources in the psychoeducational group to process all of the thoughts and emotions that may arise. You are encouraged to take notes about your thoughts and feelings, to share with your therapist.

WHAT TO EXPECT

Psychoeducational groups like this one are a unique gathering of people who are likely navigating similar life experiences, changes, or challenges. This group will meet to share these commonalities and learn, grow, and gain insight into how to better manage and improve well-being. Psychoeducational groups and workshops can be a powerful and valuable venue for discovery, growth, healing, empowerment, and hope. Your facilitating therapist will work to maintain an atmosphere of peer support that encourages open expression of concerns, challenges, and needs, while learning about the subject of evangelical Christian purity culture.

Sessions are 90 minutes in length and will occur biweekly for a period of 14 weeks. Sessions will meet each *(enter date and time)*. The meeting place address is *(enter address)*. Workshop sessions will begin on time and each member is asked to be courteous of others in terms of their promptness.

POTENTIAL RISKS AND BENEFITS OF PSYCHOEDUCATIONAL GROUPS

Participating in a psychoeducational group can result in several benefits to you. These include a better understanding of how to achieve your personal goals, improve your personal relationships, and resolve the specific challenges you are facing. It is important to recognize that this curriculum and the workshops scheduled for its delivery are not magic, and positive change does not occur overnight. Your willingness to engage fully in the group activities will play a role in how much you gain from your experience. The more open, honest, and willing you are to participate in the conversation and activities, the more you will benefit from this experience. You are welcome to share as much or as little about yourself as you feel comfortable. Please note that there can also be some discomfort in participating in a psychoeducational group/workshop. At times you may experience anxiety, sadness, frustration, or other unpleasant feelings. These emotions are both normal and expected and are simply part of the process. If these emotions are particularly bothersome, it may be helpful to discuss them with your individual/couples therapist.

CONFIDENTIALITY

Your facilitating therapist recognizes confidentiality as an ethical and legal mandate. Under most circumstances, all information about you, in written or verbal form, obtained in the psychoeducational group process (including your identity as a participant), will be kept confidential. Information will not be disclosed to any outside person(s) or agency without your written permission. However, confidentiality is not absolute and has limitations required by law. These include, but are not limited to:

1. If you are determined to be in imminent danger of harming yourself or someone else.
2. If you disclose physical or emotional abuse or neglect of a child, or an elderly or disabled person(s).
3. Where otherwise legally required.

OTHER LIMITATIONS TO CONFIDENTIALITY

Participants of the group should recognize that protecting the privacy of one another allows for an environment where trust can be built, and all members feel safe in the sharing of their experiences and questions. While there is no guarantee that all members will maintain the confidentiality of other participants, your group facilitator will monitor discussions to secure a respectful environment that keeps safety and trust a priority.

SOCIAL MEDIA

Please keep in mind that if you post an online review, status or story update, tweet, blog, or any other form of public writing, you are publicly acknowledging a therapist-client relationship, and thus waiving your right to privacy. Please consider how such a decision might impact you now or in the future.

ELECTRONIC COMMUNICATION

The facilitating therapist may communicate with you via email and/or text for general questions or concerns (such as dates and times of meetings or additional copies of activities). Email messages are not guaranteed to be confidential; cell phone companies and internet service providers retain logs of all messages and content that may be accessible to unknown persons. If you choose to text or email the facilitating therapist, you accept this potential lack of confidentiality.

GROUP CONDUCT EXPECTATIONS

To enhance our experience and allow each member to fully express themselves in a secure and affirming environment, you are asked to comply with the following expectations.

1. **Protecting one another's privacy.** It is important to feel secure in participating. This requires trust among one another. All participants agree to keep the names and identities of all other participants confidential. In the same vein, when one group member shares a personal story, asks a question, or expresses a difficult emotion, this should be held in confidence. If you would like to share another participant's experience—maybe with your partner or other members of your support system—be sure not to use anyone's name or other information that could identify that person to another.
2. **Respecting your fellow participants.** It's important that each member feel respected, valued, and supported. Please be polite; if you cannot say something kind, don't say it. Listen to what your fellow participants have to say and honor differences while celebrating connections.
3. **Honoring the process.** It is believed among psychotherapists that the more important the members consider their group to be, the more effective it becomes. Put forth the effort to participate, and to complete the activities. This will make the process more meaningful for you and for everyone involved.
4. **Attendance.** Your presence in the group is highly important. When each participant attends regularly, a group dynamic is formed to create an environment for growth and change. If you are absent from the group, this dynamic suffers and affects the experience of you and other members of the group. Therefore, you are asked to make this attendance a top priority for the duration of the group. It is understood that occasionally an emergency or unexpected event may occur that could prevent you from attending.

THE FACILITATING THERAPIST

Your group facilitating therapist is present to provide accurate information and guide the group discussion in a manner that respects all participants, allowing each member to feel respected, valued, and heard. Your facilitating therapist reserves the right to deny services to those individuals whose concerns are beyond their scope of competence or whose concerns may be better suited for individual therapy. They may also deny services to any individual who abuses or misuses services in any manner, including noncompliance with this group contract. If your facilitating therapist is unable to offer services for your specific needs, they will discuss other treatment options and possible referrals with you. Your facilitating therapist will always maintain a professional relationship with each participant. This is to protect the integrity of the therapeutic relationship as well as our mutual confidentiality and privacy. Your facilitating therapist will not accept any client invitations to connect with you, or a known family member, via Facebook, LinkedIn, Twitter, Instagram, or any other social media sites.

THERAPIST QUALIFICATIONS

Your therapist is a(n) *(insert title, degrees, qualifications et cetera)*. Their license number is *(insert license number)*.

FEES

Psychoeducational groups are a personal investment in one's overall growth and well-being. It is expected that you will pay for the services provided. *(Therapist may insert here the appropriate fees for participation, including how payment is to be provided)*.

EMERGENCIES

If you are experiencing an emergency, please contact 911 and/or go to your nearest emergency room. Calling, texting, or emailing your facilitating therapist is NOT an appropriate form of communication for such emergencies. The following numbers may also serve you in a mental health crisis:

- National Suicide Prevention Lifeline: +1 (800) 273-8255
- National Domestic Violence Hotline: +1 (800) 799-7233

Please be sure you have thoroughly reviewed this document. Your signature below indicates that you have read, understand, and agree to abide by the points outlined herein. You are encouraged to keep a copy of this document and refer to it as needed throughout your time in this psychoeducational group. Upon completion, submit it to your facilitating therapist.

DECONSTRUCTING PURITY CULTURE TO EMBRACE SEXUAL PLEASURE CONSENT FORM

I have read the above information, understand the information, and agree to the terms of psychoeducational group participation. I acknowledge that I have had the opportunity to ask questions and that such questions were answered clearly and to my satisfaction.

Signature and Date of Group Member:

_____

Printed Name of Group Member:

_____

Emergency Contact Name and Number (optional):

_____

___ I agree to be contacted by email to provide me with information pertaining to this group. Please use the following email address: _____

___ I agree to be contacted by phone to provide me information pertaining to this group. Please use the following number: _____

References

Allison, Emily J. (2021). *#Churchtoo: How purity culture upholds abuse and how to find healing*. Broadleaf Books.

Allison, Erika. (2021). *Gay the pray away: Healing your life, love, and relationships from the harms of LGBT conversion therapy*. Difference Press.

American Psychiatric Association. (2000). *Diagnostic and statistical manual of mental disorders* (4th ed.). American Psychiatric Association.

American Psychiatric Association. (2013). *Diagnostic and statistical manual of mental disorders* (5th ed.). American Psychiatric Publishing.

Anderson, D. (2015). *Damaged goods: New perspectives on Christian purity*. Jericho Books.

Anderson, L. E. (2021). *The living experience of healing the sexually traumatized self* [PhD dissertation, Saybrook University].

Ashdown, B., Hackathorn, J., & Clark, E. (2011). In and out of the bedroom: Sexual satisfaction in the marital relationship. *Journal of Integrated Social Sciences, 2*(1), 40–57. https://www.jiss.org/documents/volume_2/issue_1/JISS_2011_Sexual_Satisfaction_in_Marriage.pdf

Bader, M. (2002). *Arousal: The secret logic of sexual fantasies*. St. Martin's Press.

Bahr, H. M., & Chadwick, B. A. (1985). Religion and family in Middletown, USA. *Journal of Marriage and Family, 47*(2), 407–414. https://doi.org/10.2307/352140

Barr, B. A. (2021). *The making of Biblical womanhood: How the subjugation of women became gospel truth*. Brazos Press.

Beale, K. S., Maynard, E., & Bigler, M. O. (2016, November). *The intersection of religion and sex: Sex guilt resiliency among Baptists, Catholics, and Latter-day Saints*. Paper presented at the Society for the Scientific Study of Sexuality, Phoenix, AZ.

Beck, R. (2006). Spiritual pollution: The dilemma of sociomoral disgust and the ethic of love. *Journal of Psychology and Theology, 43*, 53–65.

Bennett, P. (1993). Critical clitoridectomy: Female sexual imagery and feminist psychoanalytic theory. *Signs: Journal of Women in Culture and Society, 18*, 235–259. https://www.doi.org/10.1086/494792

Bhavsar, V., & Bhugra, D. (2013). Cultural factors and sexual dysfunction in clinical practice. *Advances in Psychiatric Treatment, 19*(2): 144–152. https://doi.org/10.1192/apt.bp.111.009852

Binik, Y. M. (2009). The *DSM* diagnostic criteria for vaginismus. *Archives of Sexual Behavior, 39*(2), 278–291. https://doi.org/10.1007/s10508-009-9560-0

Boswell, J. (1980). *Christianity, social tolerance, and homosexuality: Gay people in Western Europe from the beginning of the Christian era to the fourteenth century.* University of Chicago Press.

Braun, V., & Kitzinger, C. (2001). "Snatch," "hole," or "honey-pot"? Semantic categories and the problem of nonspecificity in female genital slang. *Journal of Sex Research, 38*, 146–158. https://doi.org/10.1080/00224490109552082

Braun, V., & Wilkinson, S. (2001). Socio-cultural representations of the vagina. *Journal of Reproductive Health and Infant Psychology, 19*, 17–32. https://doi.org/10.1080/026483002003274

Brotto, L. A. (2018). *Better sex through mindfulness: How women can cultivate desire.* Greystone Books.

Brown, B. (2010). *The gifts of imperfection.* Hazelden Publishing.

Brown, B. (2013, January 15). Shame v. guilt [Blog post]. https://brenebrown.com/articles/2013/01/15/shame-v-guilt/

Brown, B. (2021). *Atlas of the heart: Mapping meaningful connection and the language of human experience.* Random House.

Carter, J. (2019, July 24). The FAQs: What you should know about purity culture. https://www.thegospelcoalition.org/article/faqs-know-purity-culture/

Chadwick, S. (2021). *The sweetness of Venus: A history of the clitoris.* Wild Pansy Press.

Coady, D., & Fish, N. (2011). *Healing painful sex: A woman's guide to confronting, diagnosing, and treating sexual pain.* Seal Press.

Coleman, E. (2002). Masturbation as a means of achieving sexual health. *Journal of Psychology & Human Sexuality, 14*, 5–16.

Colvin, C. (2020, November 12). This sex educator is helping people confront the effects of purity culture. Shape. https://www.shape.com

Conklin, C. (2019). Sexual attitudes and shame: Catholic women's perspectives [Doctoral dissertation, George Fox University]. https://digitalcommons.georgefox.edu/psyd/307

Conley, T. D., Moors, A. C., Matsick, J. L., Ziegler, A., & Valentine, B. A. (2011). Women, men, and the bedroom: Methodological and conceptual insights that narrow, reframe, and eliminate gender differences in sexuality. *Current Directions in Psychological Science, 20*(5), 296–300. https://doi.org/10.1177/0963721411418467

Corey, G. (2011). *Theory and practice of group counseling* (8th ed.). Brooks Cole.

Cornog, M. (1986). Naming sexual body parts: Preliminary patterns and implications. *Journal of Sex Research, 22*, 393–398. https://doi.org/10.1080/00224498609551318

Cotter, F. (2015). When tight becomes too tight: A helpful primer on vaginismus. *Jezebel.* http://jezebel.com/when-tight-becomes-too-tight-a-helpful-primer-on-vagin-1679485378

Davidson, J. K. (1984). Autoeroticism, sexual satisfaction, and sexual adjustment among university females: Past and current patterns. *Deviant Behavior, 5,* 121–140. https://doi.org/10.1080/01639625.1984.9967637

Davidson, J. K. (1995). Autoeroticism, sexual satisfaction, and sexual adjustment among university females: Past and current patterns. *Deviant Behavior, 5,* 121–140. https://doi.org/10.1080/01639625.1984.9967637

Davidson, J. K., & Darling, C. A. (1990). The influence of college-level sexuality education on female masturbatory attitudes and behaviours: A longitudinal analysis. *Australian Journal of Marriage & Family, 11*(1), 36–51.

Davidson, J. K., Darling, C. A., & Norton, L. (1995). Religiosity and the sexuality of women: Sexual behavior and sexual satisfaction revisited. *Journal of Sex Research, 32*(3), 235–243.

Davidson, J. K., Moore, N. B., & Ullstrup, K. M. (2004). Religiosity and sexual responsibility: Relationships of choice. *American Journal of Health Behavior, 28*(4), 335–346. https://www.doi.org/10.5993/AJHB.28.4.5

de Keijzer, J. (2019, March 1). Faith deconstruction: What it is and how it works [Blog post]. https://joshdekeyzer.medium.com/faith-deconstruction-what-it-is-and-how-it-works-96aca547e1e5

Definitions. (n.d.). https://transstudent.org/about/definitions/

Dobson, J. C. (1975). *What Wives Wish Their Husbands Knew About Women.* Tyndale House.

Dodson, B. (1996). *Sex for one.* Random House.

Eggerichs, E. (2004). *Love & respect: The love she most desires, the respect he desperately needs.* Integrity Publishers.

Fahs, B., & Frank, E. (2014). Notes from the back room: Gender, power, and (in)visibility in women's experiences of masturbation. *Journal of Sex Research, 51,* 241–252. https://doi.org/10.1080/00224499.2012.745474

Finch, J. L. (2019). *You are your own: A reckoning with the religious trauma of evangelical Christianity.* Self-published.

Fitzgerald, F. (2017). *The evangelicals: The struggle to shape America.* Simon & Schuster.

Fox, E., & Young, M. (1989). Religiosity, sex guilt, and sexual behavior among college students. *Health Values, 13*(2), 32–37.

Fredrickson, B. L., & Roberts, T. A. (1997). Objectification theory: Toward understanding women's lived experiences and mental health risks. *Psychology of Women Quarterly, 21*(2), 173–206. https://doi.org/10.1111/j.1471-6402.1997.tb00108.x

Gardner, C. J. (2011). *Making chastity sexy: The rhetoric of evangelical abstinence campaigns.* University of California Press.

Gartrell, N., & Mosbacher, D. (1984). Sex differences in the naming of children's genitals. *Sex Roles, 10,* 867–876. https://www.doi.org/10.1007/BF00288510

Garvin, C. D. (1996). *Contemporary group work* (3rd ed.). Pearson.

Gerber, L. (2008). The opposite of gay: Nature, creation, and Queerish ex-gay experiments. *Nova Religio, 11*(4), 8–30. https://doi.org/10.1525/nr.2008.11.4.8

Gilbert, P. (2003). Evolution, social roles, and differences in shame and guilt. *Social Research: An International Quarterly of the Social Sciences, 70*, 1205–1230. http://www.jstor.org./stable/40971967

Gilligan, C. (2003). *The birth of pleasure: A new map of love.* Vintage Books.

Graham, C. A., Sanders, S. A., & Milhausen, R. R. (2006). The sexual excitation/sexual inhibition inventory for women: psychometric properties. *Archives of Sexual Behavior, 35*(4), 397–409. https://doi.org/10.1007/s10508-006-9041-7

Graziottin, A. (2006). Sexual pain disorders: Dyspareunia and vaginismus. In H. Porst & J. Buvat (Eds.), *Standard practice in sexual medicine* (pp. 342–350). Blackwell.

Graziottin, A., & Murina, F. (2011a). Vulvodynia and dyspareunia: How should they be addressed? In A. Graziottin & F. Murina (Eds.), *Clinical Management of Vulvodynia* (pp.15-27). Springer

Graziottin, A., & Murina, F. (2011b). Epidemiology of vulvar pain and its sexual comorbidities. In A. Graziottin & F. Murina (Eds.), *Clinical Management of Vulvodynia* (pp. 1–5). Springer.

Gregoire, S. W., Lindenbach, R. G., & Sawatsky, J. (2021). *The great sex rescue: The lies you've been taught and how to recover what god intended.* Baker Books.

Gudorf, C. (1994). *Body, sex, and pleasure: Reconstructing Christian sexual ethics.* Pilgrim Press.

Hardy, J. W., & Easton, D. (2017). *The ethical slut.* Crown Publishing.

Harris, J., (1997). *I kissed dating goodbye.* Multnomah Publishers.

Hart, D. G. (2002). *That old-time religion in modern America: Evangelical Protestantism in the twentieth century.* Ivan R. Dee.

Hastings, A. S. (1998). *Treating sexual shame: A new map for overcoming dysfunction, abuse, and addiction.* Jason Aronson.

Hawton, K., & Catalan, J. (2007). Sex therapy for vaginismus: Characteristics of couples and treatment outcome. *Sexual and Marital Therapy, 5*(1), 39–48. https://doi.org/10.1080/02674659008407995

Helgeson, V. S., & Fritz, H. L. (1999). Unmitigated agency and unmitigated communion: Distinctions from agency and communion. *Journal of Research in Personality, 33*, 131–158. https://doi.org/10.1006/jrpe.1999.2241

Hendrick, C., Hendrick, S., & Reich, D. (2006). The Brief Sexual Attitudes Scale. *Journal of Sex Research, 43*, 76–86. https://doi.org/10.1080/00224490609552301

Herbenick, D., Reece, M., Schick, V., Sanders, S. A., Dodge, B., & Fortenberry, J. D. (2010). Sexual behavior in the United States: Results from a national probability sample of men and women ages 14–94. *Journal of Sexual Medicine, 7*, 255–265. https://www.doi.org/10.1111/j.1743-6109.2010.02012.x

Hirst, J., Baggaley, M., & Watson, J. (1996). A four-year survey of an inner-city psychosexual problems clinic. *Sexual and Marital Therapy, 11*(1), 19–36. https://doi.org/10.1080/02674659608404281

Hungrige, A. (2016). Women's masturbation: An exploration of the influence of shame, guilt, and religiosity [Doctoral dissertation, Texas Woman's University]. https://twu-ir.tdl.org/handle/11274/8755

Impett, E. A., Schooler, D., & Tolman, D. L. (2006). To be seen and not heard: Femininity ideology and adolescent girls' sexual health. *Archives of Sexual Behavior, 35*(2), 129–142. https://doi.org/10.1007/s10508-005-9016-0

Ingersoll, J. (2003). *Evangelical Christian women: War stories in the gender battles.* New York University Press.

Kinsey Institute. (n.d.). Dual control model of sexual response. https://kinseyinstitute.org/research/dual-control-model.php

Klein, L. K. (2018). *Pure: Inside the evangelical movement that shamed a generation of young women and how I broke free.* Atria Books.

Klein, M. (2012). *Sexual intelligence: What we really want from sex and how to get it.* HarperCollins.

Kleinplatz, P., & Menard, D. A. (2020). *Magnificent sex: Lessons from extraordinary lovers.* Routledge.

Knowles, J. (2002). *Masturbation: From stigma to sexual health* [White paper]. Planned Parenthood. https://www.plannedparenthood.org/uploads/filer _public/8e/f5/8ef53e54-2fcb-4f92-933e-59fa0a09285b/masturbation_11-02.pdf

Kobes Du Mez, K. (2020). *Jesus and John Wayne: How white evangelicals corrupted a faith and fractured a nation.* Liveright Publishing Corporation.

LaHaye, T. (2002). *How to be happy though married.* Tyndale House Publishers.

Laumann, E. O., Gagnon, J. H., Michael, R. T., & Michaels, S. (1994). *The social organization of sexuality: Sexual practices in the United States.* University of Chicago Press.

Lerner, H. (2004). *Fear and other uninvited guests: Tackling the anxiety, fear, and shame that keep us from optimal living and loving.* HarperCollins.

Lerner, H. E. (1977). Parental mislabeling of female genitals as a determinant of penis envy and learning inhibitions in women. In H. P. Blum (Ed.), *Female psychology: Contemporary psychoanalytic views* (pp. 269–283). International Universities Press.

Levine, S. B., Althof, S. E., & Risen, C. B. (2016). *Handbook of clinical sexuality for mental health professionals.* Routledge.

Lewis, R. W., Fugl-Meyer, K. S., Bosch, R., Fugl-Meyer, A. R., Laumann, E. O., Lizza, E., & Martin-Morales, A. (2004). Epidemiology/risk factors of sexual dysfunction. *Journal of Sexual Medicine, 1*(1), 35–39. https://doi.org/10.1111/j .1743-6109.2004.10106.x

Lifeway. (n.d.). True love waits: History. https://www.lifeway.com/en/product -family/true-love-waits

Lloyd, E. A. (2005). *The case of the female orgasm: Bias in the science of evolution.* Harvard University Press.

Lovett, I. (2013, June 20). After 37 years of trying to change people's sexual orientation, group is to disband. *New York Times.* https://www.nytimes.com

Malcolm, C., & Golsworthy, R. (2019). Working relationally with clients who have experienced abuse: Exploring counselling psychologists' experiences using IPA. *European Journal of Counselling Psychology, 8*(1), 144–162.

Marcinechová, D., & Záhorcová, L. (2020). Sexual satisfaction, sexual attitudes, and shame in relation to religiosity. *Sexuality & Culture, 24*(6), 1913–1928. https://doi.org/10.1007/s12119-020-09727-3

Martin, B. (2021). *The art of receiving and giving: The wheel of consent.* Luminare Press.

McCarthy, B. W. (2015). *Sex made simple: Clinical strategies for sexual issues in therapy.* PESI Publishing & Media LLC.

McCleneghan, B. (2011). *Good Christian sex: Why chastity isn't the only option and other things the Bible says about sex.* HarperCollins.

McClintock, K. A. (2001). *Sexual shame: An urgent call to healing.* Augsburg Fortress.

McCool-Myers, M., Theurich, M., Zuelke, A., Knuettel, H., & Apfelbacher, C. (2018). Predictors of female sexual dysfunction: A systematic review and qualitative analysis through gender inequality paradigms. *BMC Women's Health, 18*(1). https://doi.org/10.1186/s12905-018-0602-4

McGrath, A. E. (1996). *Evangelicalism and the future of Christianity.* Hodder & Stoughton.

Michael, R. T., Gagnon, J. H., Laumann, E. O., & Kolata, G. (1994). *Sex in America: A definitive survey.* Little, Brown.

Mills, R. (2004). Taking stock of the developmental literature on shame. *Developmental Review, 25,* 26–63. https://doi.org/10.1016/j.dr.2004.08.001

Mintz, L. (2017). *Becoming cliterate: Why orgasm equality matters—and how to get it.* HarperCollins.

Mizrahi, M. (2018). *Culture, religion, and vaginismus* [PhD dissertation, California School of Professional Psychology].

Moslener, S. (2015). *Virgin nation: Sexual purity and American adolescence.* Oxford University Press.

Muise, A., Preyde, M., Maitland, S. B., & Milhausen, R. R. (2010). Sexual identity and sexual well-being in female heterosexual university students. *Archives of Sexual Behavior, 39*(4), 915–925. https://doi.org/10.1007/s10508-009-9492-8

Murray, K. M., Ciarrocchi, J. W., & Murray-Swank, N. A. (2007). Spirituality, religiosity, shame and guilt as predictors of sexual attitudes and experiences. *Journal of Psychology and Theology, 35*(3), 222–234. https://doi.org/10.1177/009164710703500305

Nagoski, E. (2015a). *Come as you are: The surprising new science that will transform your sex life.* Simon & Schuster.

Nagoski, E. (2015b). Turning off the offs. https://static1.squarespace.com/static/5a2311d41f318d2a02e64554/t/6041267ed050703aae57b69f/1614882431026/TURNING%2BOFF%2BTHE%2BOFFS%2BWORKSHEETS.pdf

Nagoski, E. (2021). *Come as you are: The surprising new science that will transform your sex life* (2nd. ed.). Simon & Schuster Paperbacks.

Nagoski, E. (2024). *Come together: The science (and art!) of creating lasting sexual connections.* Ballantine Books.

Ogden, G. (2008). *The return of desire: A guide to rediscovering your sexual passion.* Trumpeter Books.

Ogletree, S. M., & Ginsburg, H. J. (2000). Kept under the hood: Neglect of the clitoris in common vernacular. *Sex Roles, 43*(11/12), 917–926. https://doi.org/10.1023/a:1011093123517

Ogren, D. (1974). *Sexual guilt, behavior, attitudes, and information* [Doctoral dissertation, University of Houston]. https://hdl.handle.net/10657/11796

Oxford Online Dictionary. (2021a). Guilt. https://en.oxforddictionaries.com/definition/guilt

Oxford Online Dictionary. (2021b). Shame. https://en.oxforddictionaries.com/definition/shame

Patton, M. S. (1985). Masturbation from Judaism to Victorianism. *Journal of Religious Health, 24*, 133–146. https://doi.org/10.1007/BF01532257

Pew Research Center. (2015, May 11). America's changing religious landscape. https://www.pewforum.org/2015/05/12/americas-changing-religious-landscape/

Pitts, M., & Rahman, Q. (2001). Which behaviors constitute "having sex" among university students in the UK? *Archives of Sexual Behavior, 30*, 169–176. https://www.doi.org/ 10.1023/A:1002777201416

Prentice, D. A., & Carranza, E. (2002). What women and men should be, shouldn't be, are allowed to be, and don't have to be: The contents of prescriptive gender stereotypes. *Psychology of Women Quarterly, 26*, 269–281. https://journals.sagepub.com/doi/pdf/10.1111/1471-6402.t01-1-00066

Reissing, E. D., Binik, Y. M., Khalife, S., Cohen, D., & Amsel, R. (2003). Vaginal spasm, pain, and behavior: An empirical investigation of the diagnosis of vaginismus. *Archives of Sexual Behavior, 33*(1). https://doi.org/10.1023/B:ASEB.0000007458.32852.c8

Rethinking Schools. (2020, June 9). A look at the "sex respect" curriculum. https://rethinkingschools.org/articles/a-look-at-the-sex-respect-curriculum/

Roberts, M. (2020). *Beyond shame: Creating a healthy sex life on your own terms*. Fortress Press.

Rosenbloom, S. (2005, December 8). A ring that says no, not yet. *New York Times*. https://www.nytimes.com/2005/12/08/fashion/thursdaystyles/a-ring-that-says-no-not-yet.html

Russo, M. D. (2021, March 24). 3 great lubes that are safe to use with silicone sex toys. *Mic*. https://www.mic.com/p/the-3-best-lubes-for-silicone-sex-toys-22627393

Sanders, S. A., & Reinisch, J. M. (1999). Would you say you "had sex" if . . . ? *Journal of the American Medical Association, 281*(3), 275–277. https://doi.org/10.1001/jama.281.3.275

Saul, R. (1998, April 01). *Whatever happened to the Adolescent Family Life Act?* Guttmacher Institute. https://www.guttmacher.org/gpr/1998/04/whatever-happened-to-the-adolescent-family-life-act

Sellers, T. S. (2017). *Sex, God, and the conservative church: Erasing shame from sexual intimacy*. Routledge.

Sex Respect Student Workbook. (2019, April 26). https://avemariaradio.net/product/sex-respect-student-workbook/

Simonelli, C., Eleuteri, S., Petruccelli, F., & Rossi, R. (2014). Female sexual pain disorders: dyspareunia and vaginismus. *Current Opinion in Psychiatry, 27*(6), 406–412.

Simpson, W. S., & Ramberg, J. A. (1992). The influence of religion on sexuality: Implications for sex therapy. In R. Green (Ed.), *Religion and sexual health* (pp. 155–165). Springer. https://doi.org/10.1007/978-94-015-7963-6_9

Smith, E. (2020). My sexual values workbook: A purity culture dropout resource. https://www.ericasmitheac.com/webinars-books/p/my-sexual-values-workbook-a-purity-culture-dropout-resource

Spector, I. P., & Carey, M. P. (1990). Incidence and prevalence of the sexual dysfunctions: A critical review of the empirical literature. *Archives of Sexual Behavior, 19*(4), 389–408. https://doi.org/10.1007/bf01541933

Substance abuse and mental health services administration. SAMHSA. (n.d.). https://www.samhsa.gov/

Sweeney, D. A. (2005). *The American evangelical story: A history of the movement.* Baker Academic.

Swindle, P. (2017). *A Twisting of the Sacred* [Doctoral dissertation, University of North Carolina]. https://www.proquest.com/openview/2f8757f55d11975590c5affc36b72169/1?pqorigsite=gscholar&cbl=18750&diss=y

Sznycer, D., Takemura, K., Delton, A. W., Sato, K., Robertson, T., Cosmides, L., & Tooby, J. (2012). Cross-cultural differences and similarities in proneness to shame: An adaptationist and ecological approach. *Evolutionary Psychology, 10,* 352–370.

Tangney, J. P., & Dearing, R. L. (2003). *Shame and guilt* (1st ed.). Guilford Press.

ter Kuile, M. M., Bulté, I., Weijenborg, P. T. M., Beekman, A., Melles, R., & Onghena, P. (2009). Therapist-aided exposure for women with lifelong vaginismus: A replicated single-case design. *Journal of Consulting and Clinical Psychology, 77*(1), 149–159. http://psycnet.apa.org/doi/10.1037/a0014273

Tiefer, L. (1996). Towards a feminist sex therapy. *Women and Therapy, 19,* 53–64. https://www.doi.org/ 10.1300/J015v19n04_07

Tolman, D. L. (2002). *Dilemmas of desire: Teenage girls talk about sexuality.* Harvard University Press.

Tolman, D. L., & Porsche, M. V. (2000). The Adolescent Femininity Ideology Scale: Development and validation of a new measure for girls. *Psychology of Women Quarterly, 24,* 365–376. https://doi.org/10.1111/j.1471-6402.2000.tb00219.x

2014 American Counseling Association Code of Ethics. (2014). https://www.counseling.org/docs/default-source/default-document-library/ethics/2014-aca-code-of-ethics.pdf?sfvrsn=55ab73d0_1

Valenti, J. (2010). *The purity myth: How America's obsession with virginity is hurting young women.* Seal Press.

Ward, E., & Ogden, J. (1994). Experiencing vaginismus—Sufferers beliefs about causes and effects. *Sexual and Marital Therapy, 9*(1), 33–45. https://doi.org/10.1080/02674659408409565

Weeks, J. (1989). *Sexuality.* Routledge.

West, S. L., Vinikoor, L. C., & Zolnoun, D. (2004). A systematic review of the literature on female sexual dysfunction prevalence and predictors. *Annual Review of Sex Research, 15,* 40–172.

Winell, M. (1993). *Leaving the fold: A guide for former fundamentalists and others leaving their religion.* Apocryphile Press.

Wise, N. (2019). *Why good sex matters: Understanding the neuroscience of pleasure for smarter, happier, and more purpose-filled life.* Houghton Mifflin Harcourt.

Woo, J. S. T. (2001). *Mechanisms that underlie cultural disparities in women's sexual desire: The role of sex guilt and its treatment* [Unpublished dissertation, University of British Columbia]. https://open.library.ubc.ca/cIRcle/collections/ubctheses/24/items/1.0073574

Index

abortion, false information about, 70
abstinence, 58; before marriage,
9–10; religion-based movements
prioritizing, ix; Silver Ring Thing
promoting, 33
abstinence campaigns, 31
Abstinence Clearinghouse (nonprofit),
71
abstinence groups, 37
abstinence-only education, 71; Bush
advocating for, 30–31; in public
schools, 33, 70; state school systems
investing in, 69
abstinence pledge card, 31–32
abuse, 21–22, 59; misogyny and, 92;
in relationships, 12–13; sexual, 5–7,
53–54
adolescent development, female, 103–4
Adolescent Family Life Act (AFLA),
30, 68
alienation from God, sexual shame
linked with, 41, 87
Allen, Steve, 123
Allison, Erika, 58, 86, 87

American Association of Sexuality
Educators, Counselors and
Therapists, 125
American Counseling Association
Code of Ethics, 27
American Medical Association, 115
American Psychiatric Association, 59
anatomy, *111*, *113*
Anderson, Dianna, 26, 34, 40, 68–69,
86, 96; *Damaged Goods* by, 36, 72;
"impure" girls discussed by, 85;
on purity culture, 92, 95; on purity
movement, 70; on sex and guilt,
74; on sexuality, 41, 88; shame
discussed by, 87
Anderson, Laura, 21
anxiety: the body holding onto,
48; about right and wrong, 5;
vaginismus and, 51
attendance, 134
attention, sex and, 53–54
Augustine, 73, 116
autonomy, bodily, 6

Bader, Michael, 103
Balmer, Randall, 93
Bancroft, John, 106
Barr, B. A., 66, 91
Beale, K. S., 38, 74
becoming, journey of, 4
Becoming Cliterate (Mintz), 25, 115
Bennett, Paula, 117
Better Sex Through Mindfulness (Brotto), 100
Bible, translating, 4
biblical courtship, 69
birth control, 9, 70
BMC Women's Health study, 43
bodily autonomy, 6
the body: anxiety held onto in, 48; girls not exploring, 37; sexuality associated with, 24; sin and, 37. *See also* clitoris
books, on purity culture, 126
born again, 67
Brotto, Lori A., 100
Brown, Brené, 39, 78, 79, 84
Bush, George W., 30–31

Carter, Joe, 30, 68
Catalan, J., 47
CDC. *See* Centers for Disease Control and Prevention
celibacy, 58, 94–95
Centers for Disease Control and Prevention (CDC), 30
Chadwick, S., 112
childbirth, 112
Christian church, evangelical. *See* evangelical Christian church
Christian college, 11
#Churchtoo (Allison), 86
cisgender, 90
clinical sexology, 15, 22–23
clitoral stimulation, vaginal penetration compared with, 117
clitoris: anatomy of, *113*; pleasure created in, 112; silence on, 110
codependency, sexual, 103
Coleman, E., 84
Come as You Are (Nagoski), 25–26, 66, 107

complementarianism, 91–92
comprehensive sex education, Obama funding, 30–31
conduct expectations, group, 134
confidentiality, 133
Conklin, Colleen, 87
consent, 65
consent forms, 136
conversion therapy, 59, 94–95
core beliefs, of purity culture, 65
couples' therapists, 13
courtship, biblical, 69
culture shock, 11

Damaged Goods (Anderson), 36, 72
dancing, 8
dating, 8–9
Davidson, J. Kenneth, 116
deconstruction, 19–20, 27, 64, 65–66, 125, 131
Denton, Jeremiah, 30, 68
desire, 49, 99, 104; Nagoski on, 102; spiritual aspects of, 103; spontaneous contrasted with responsive, 45, 101–2
Diagnostic and Statistical Manual of Mental Disorders (American Medical Association), 43, 115
discussion, 97–98
discussion questions, 75, 81, 88, 107–8, 121
divorce, 6–7
Dobson, James, 36–37, 73, 93–94
Dodson, Betty, 116
domesticity, 93
domestic life, evangelical Christians concerned with, 70–71
dual control model, pleasure explained through, 106
dyspareunia, 46

Easton, D., 65, 84
education, abstinence-only. *See* abstinence-only education
education, comprehensive sex, 30–31
Eggerichs, E., 44
electronic communication, 133–34

Elliot, Elizabeth, 69
emergencies, 135–36
emotional purity, 72
ethics, sexual, 95–96
evangelical Christian church,
    ix–x, 4–5, 68, 97, 115–16, 118–19;
    hypersexualized culture reacted
    to by, 31; LGBTQIA+ community
    impacted by, 57–58; purity culture
    and, 15–17; second or renewed
    virginity offered by, 37; separation
    of church and state disassembled
    by, 71; sex-negative messages
    developed by, 35, 70; sex therapists
    discussing, 16; sexual shame taught
    through, 85; silence encouraged by,
    41; women oppressed by, 92
evangelical Christianity, in United
    States, 19
evangelical Christians, domestic life
    concerning, 70–71
evangelicalism, 68; gender distinctions
    within, 37; Protestant reforms
    as root of, 29, 67; same-sex
    relationships challenging, 94; sexual
    dysfunction and, 44
*Evangelicalism and the Future of
    Christianity* (McGrath), 29, 68
Exodus International, 59, 94–95

facilitating therapists, 134–35
faith, sexuality combined with, 64
family values, traditional, 93
fathers, 69
fees, 135
female adolescent development, 103–4
female genitalia, 110–14
female sexual anatomy, 113–14
female sexual dysfunction, 43, 101
female sexuality: commodification
    of, 73; Dobson describing, 36–37;
    shame and, 110
Finch, Jamie Lee, 25, 37, 74
First Great Awakening, 67
Focus on the Family (ministry), 36–37,
    69, 93
Fox, E., 40, 79
friendships, 58–59

garden exercise, 124–25
gatekeepers of sexuality, women as,
    40, 85, 91, 118
Gay the Pray Away (Allison), 58
gender distinctions, within
    evangelicalism, 37
gender divide, 92
gender expression/presentation, 90
gender identity, 90
gender roles, 93; Dobson believing
    in, 94; for men, 89–90; sexual
    dysfunction linked with, 48–49
genitalia, female, 110–14
Gilbert, Paul, 41, 87
Ginsburg, H. J., 110
girls: the body not explored by, 37;
    "good," 103; "impure," 85; purity
    culture focusing on teenage, 74;
    sexual pleasure not explored by, 37
God, sexual shame linked with
    alienation from, 41, 87
Golsworthy, R., 22
"good girls," 103
Gregoire, Sheila Wray, 25, 44, 91, 118
Grenz, Stanley, 58
Gresh, Dannah, 32–33
grief, deconstruction and, 125
ground rules, 64–67
group conduct expectations, 134
G-spot, 120
guided mediation, 126–27
guilt, 24; Anderson, D., on sex, 74;
    sex, 79; shame contrasted with, 78

Hardy, J. W., 65, 84
Harris, Josh, 69
Hart, D. G., 67
Hatch, Orrin, 30, 68
Hawton, K., 47
healing, 3–4, 23, 61
Hester, Jimmy, 31–32
heterosexual, 90
heterosexual marriage, sexual
    expression outside, 6–7
history, of purity culture, 65
holy living, 67
homework, 74–75, 81–82, 88, 98, 108,
    121

honeymoons, 51
honoring the process, 134
How to Be Happy Though Married (LaHaye), 92
Hungrige, A., 84
hypersexualized culture, evangelical Christian church reacting to, 31

I Kissed Dating Goodbye (Harris), 69
"impure" girls, Anderson, D., on, 85
inauthenticity, in relationships, 104
Indiana University, National Survey of Sexual Health and Behavior from, 115
informed consent, 27
Ingersoll, J., 37
intelligence, sexual, 96–97
intimacy, 45

Janssen, Erik, 106

Kinsey Institute, 106
kissing, 8
Klein, Linda Kay, 25, 71, 83, 85
Klein, Marty, 96, 114
Kleinplatz, Peggy, 101
Knowles, Jon, 117
Kobes Du Mez, K., 69, 90, 92–93

LaHaye, Beverly, 92–93
LaHaye, Tim, 92–93
Lerner, Harriet, 110
lesbian, gay, bisexual, trans, queer, questioning, intersex, asexual, aromantic, pansexual, polysexual (LGBTQIAPP+), 90
LGBTQIA+ community, 6; celibacy forced on, 94–95; conversion therapy impacting, 59; evangelical Christian church impacting, 57–58
LGBTQIAPP+. *See* lesbian, gay, bisexual, trans, queer, questioning, intersex, asexual, aromantic, pansexual, polysexual
Lifeway (publisher), 31, 68
lived experiences, of sex-negative messages, 129

Lloyd, Elisabeth, 117–18
Love & Respect (Eggerichs), 44
lube, sex toys and, 119–21
lust, 86

Magnificent Sex (Kleinplatz and Menard), 101
Malcolm, C., 22
male headship, 92
marriage, 13–14; abstinence before, 9–10; hierarchical view of, 44–45; high value placed on, 11; sex outside of, 9; sexual expression outside heterosexual, 6–7; virgin status before, 25
masturbate, how to, 117–18
masturbation, 117; Ogden supporting, 73; OMG Yes and, 118; sex-negative messages influencing, 114; sin and, 115–16
"Masturbation" (white paper), 117
McCarthy, Barry, 52
McCleneghan, Bromleigh, 71, 73
McGrath, Alister, 29, 30, 68
mediation, guided, 126–27
men, 91; gender roles for, 89–90; protection and, 7–8; roles of, 70–71
Menard, Dana, 101
mental health practitioners, 20–22, 34, 42, 129
mental health professionals, religious indoctrination worked with by, 63–64
middle school, sexual education in, 9
Mills, Rosemary, 39, 79
mindfulness, 99–100
Mintz, Laurie, 25, 115
misogyny, abuse and, 92
modesty, 7, 40, 69, 86
Mohler, Albert, 31
mons pubis, 112
Moslener, Sara, 36–37, 73

Nagoski, Emily, 45, 96, 100–101; *Come as You Are* by, 25–26, 66, 107; on desire, 102; on orgasm, 113–14; pleasure defined by, 104–5

National Association of Evangelicals, 68
National Domestic Violence Hotline, 135
National Longitudinal Study of Adolescent Health, 33
National Mall, pledge cards displayed on, 32
National Suicide Prevention Lifeline, 135
National Survey of Sexual Attitudes and Lifestyles (NATSAL), 101
National Survey of Sexual Health and Behavior, from Indiana University, 115
NATSAL. *See* National Survey of Sexual Attitudes and Lifestyles
negative experiences, pleasure held back by, 98
neuropathways, 21
Newsweek (magazine), 19

Obama, Barack, 30–31
objectives, 63–64, 77–78, 82–84, 89, 99–100, 109, 123
Ogden, Gina, 73, 94, 102–3
Ogden, J., 48
Ogletree, S. M., 110
Ogren, D., 79
OMG Yes (website), 25, 118
Onan, story of (Book of Genesis), 115–16
onanism, 116
orgasm, 49, 113–14
"other," fear of being, 97
Oxford Online Dictionary, 78, 79

pain: during penetrative sex, 14, 50–51; sexual, 43. *See also* sexual dysfunction
pain disorders, vaginal, 46
Papua New Guinea, 4, 7, 9–10
parents, 53–55
participants, benefits to, 24–26
Patton, Michael, 115
Pattyn, Amy, 33
Pattyn, Denny, 33

Paul (apostle), 85–86
PC. *See* pubococcygeus
peer pressure, 10
pelvic floor physical therapist, 14, 52
penetrative sex, pain during, 14, 50–51
physical therapist, pelvic floor, 14, 52
Planned Parenthood, 117
pleasure, 49, 52, 86, 107; as birthright, 130; clitoris creating, 112; dual control model explaining, 106; healing achieving, 23; Nagoski defining, 104–5; negative experiences holding back, 98
pledge cards: abstinence, 31–32; Abstinence Clearinghouse selling, 71; National Mall displaying, 32; purity, 10
pornography, 118–19
pregnancy, teen, 54
privacy: protecting, 134; right to, 133
protection, men and, 7–8
Protestant reforms, evangelicalism rooted in, 29, 67
psychoeducational groups, risks and benefits of, 132
puberty, 7, 53
public schools, abstinence-only education in, 33, 70
pubococcygeus (PC), 46, 47
Pure Freedom, 32–33
purity, 33
purity balls, Focus on the Family originating, 69
purity culture. *See specific topics*
The Purity Myth (Valenti), 36–37, 72
purity pledge cards, 10
purity pledges, sexual behaviors not impacted by, 70
purity rings, 10, 32

queer, 90
the raisin (mindfulness exercise), 100–101

Ramberg, J. A., 44
rape, in Papua New Guinea, 7
Reagan, Ronald, 68

relationships, 12–13, 104
religion, 84, 105; dogmatic, 20–21, 63–64; sexual expression limited by, 97; sexuality and, 22; silence and, 129. *See also* evangelical Christian church
religion-based movements, abstinence prioritized by, ix
religious indoctrination, mental health professionals working with, 63–64
religious sexual shame, 40
respect, 134
responsibilities, boyfriends and, 8–9
responsive desire, spontaneous desire contrasted with, 45, 101–2
The Return of Desire (Ogden), 102
right to privacy, 133
rings, purity, 10, 32
Roberts, Matthias, 79, 80–81, 88
romantic love, 71
Ross, Richard, 31–32, 68–69

same-sex attraction, 9, 14–15
same-sex relationships, evangelicalism challenged by, 94
SAMHSA. *See* Substance Abuse and Mental Health Services Administration
Saturday Night Live, 33
school systems, state, 69
SE. *See* sexual excitation system
second or renewed virginity, evangelical Christian church offering, 37
self-efficacy, sexual, 104
self-exploration, 73
Sellers, Tina, 37–38, 41, 87, 116
separation of church and state, evangelical Christian church disassembling, 71
sex, 45; Anderson on guilt, 74; attention and, 53–54; lack of interest in, 54; outside of marriage, 9; pain during penetrative, 50–51; presence lacked during, 54–55; scripts or narratives about, 102–3; sin and, 73. *See also* masturbation

Sex, God, and the Conservative Church (Sellers), 37–38, 116
sex education, comprehensive, 30–31
sex guilt, 79
Sex Has a Price Tag, 70
sex-negative messages: of evangelical Christian church, 35, 70; lived experiences of, 129; masturbation influenced by, 114
sexology, clinical, 15
Sex Respect (program), 30
Sex Respect Student Workbook, 68
sex therapists, 3, 15, 24, 34, 42, 129; evangelical Christian church discussed by, 16; looking for, 23; vaginismus treated with, 46–47
sex toys, lube and, 119–21
sexual abuse, 5–7, 53–54
sexual anatomy, female, 113–14
sexual and psychological effects, of purity culture, 38
sexual behaviors, purity pledges not impacting, 70
sexual codependency, 103
sexual dysfunction: evangelicalism and, 44; female, 43, 101; gender roles linked with, 48–49; shame influencing, 50
sexual education, in middle school, 9
sexual ethics, 95–96
sexual excitation system (SE), 106
sexual expression: healing achieving, 23; outside heterosexual marriage, 6–7; religion limiting, 97
sexual inhibition system (SI), 106
sexual intelligence, 96–97
sexuality, 5, 15, 23, 126; Anderson, D., on, 41, 88; the body associated with, 24; faith combined with, 64; female, 110; purity culture restricting, 49–50; religion and, 22; women as gatekeepers of, 40, 85, 91, 118. *See also* female sexuality
sexually transmitted infections (STI), 9, 70
sexual orientation, 90
sexual pain, 43

sexual pleasure. *See specific topics*
sexual self-efficacy, 104
sexual shame, 39; alienation from God linked with, 41, 87; definition of, 84; evangelical Christian church teaching, 85; religious, 40; research lacked around, 83–84
shame, 24, 77–78, 80–81; Anderson, D., discussing, 87; female sexuality and, 110; guilt contrasted with, 78; purity culture and, 83; sexual dysfunction influenced by, 50
shamelessness, 80
shaming language, 102
showers, 108
SI. *See* sexual inhibition system
silence, 41, 91–92, 110, 129
silicone, 120–21
Silver Ring Thing (organization), 33, 58
Simpson, W. S., 44
sin, 6–7; the body and, 37; masturbation and, 115–16; women and, 25, 32
social media, 133
Southern Baptist Convention, 68
splitting, 102
spontaneous desire, responsive desire contrasted with, 45, 101–2
state school systems, abstinence-only education invested in by, 69
STI. *See* sexually transmitted infections
story of Onan (Book of Genesis), 115–16
Substance Abuse and Mental Health Services Administration (SAMHSA), 21–22
Sweeney, Douglas, 29, 67
Swindle, Paula, 22

teenage girls, purity culture focusing on, 74
teen pregnancy, 30, 54, 74
Tiefer, Leonore, 110
touch, five gears of, 52
ToyLife foaming toy cleaner, 120

traditional family values, 93
trauma-informed care, 21–22
True Love Waits campaign, 9–10, 31–32, 58, 68–69

UCLA, Williams Institute at, 59
United States, evangelical Christianity in, 19

vaginal canal, 112
vaginal dilation, 47–48
vaginal pain disorders, 46
vaginal penetration, clitoral stimulation compared with, 117–18
vaginal tenting, 111
vaginismus, 46–47, 51
Valenti, Jessica, 36–37, 72
virginity, 37, 72
Virgin Nation (Moslener), 36–37, 73
virgin status, before marriage, 25
vulva, 110–12, 121
vulva anatomy, *111*
vulvodynia, 46

Ward, E., 48
wedding nights, 25, 50
weeding your garden, 66–67
Weeks, Jeffrey, 39, 84
Welfare Reform Act (1996), 30–31
West, S. L., 43
What Wives Wish Their Husbands Knew About Women (Dobson), 93
When Harry Met Sally (movie), 114
Why Good Sex Matters (Wise), 118
wifely duty, 119
Williams Institute, at UCLA, 59
Winell, M., 78
Wise, Nan, 105–6, 118
women, 43, 93; evangelical Christian church oppressing, 92; as gatekeepers of sexuality, 40, 85, 91, 118; purity movement impacting, 86; roles of, 70–71; sin and, 25, 32. *See also* girls

Young, M., 40, 79, 85

About the Author

Andreya Jones grew up in a conservative, evangelical community in Papua New Guinea and Senegal, West Africa. She began her career in psychology as a case manager who worked with sexually abused children. After obtaining her master's degree in social work, she worked with troubled teens and their families before entering the world of private practice. Andreya has a doctorate in clinical sexology, is a licensed clinical social worker, and is an AASECT certified sex therapist who owns a private practice in Pennsylvania. In the process of deconstructing from Christian evangelicalism and becoming the person she was meant to be, she has devoted her time and energy to helping other women who have had similar experiences. She is passionate about helping clients navigate their relationships, sexuality, and pleasure. Andreya has the privilege of living with and loving her two rambunctious kids and fur babies. She is grateful to be building a new life with her love of lifetimes.

www.ingramcontent.com/pod-product-compliance
Lightning Source LLC
Chambersburg PA
CBHW062036270326
41929CB00014B/2447